EMBRACE YOUR CROWN

A TIME MANAGEMENT HANDBOOK

Ordering Information:
For quantity sales, Trient Press offers special discounts to corporations, associations, and other organizations. For detailed information, contact the publisher at the address provided above.
For orders by U.S. trade bookstores and wholesalers, please reach out to Trient Press at Tel: (775) 996-3844, or visit www.trientpress.com.

Printed in the United States of America

Publisher's Cataloging-in-Publication Data

Carter, Trenace
Embrace Your Crown: A Time Management Handbook

- Hardcover: ISBN 979-8-88990-158-7

- Paperback: ISBN 979-8-88990-159-4

- E-book: ISBN 979-8-88990-160-0

The Essence of a Black Queen

Chapter 1

Imagine, if you will, the dawn's first rays splaying out across a bustling city. The world is just shaking off the tendrils of slumber, yawning into existence once again. Yet, before the urban landscape is fully awake, a chorus of the unbreakable, the resilient, and the dauntless is already filling the air - the Black women of our communities, pouring their energy into the new day.

Their strength goes beyond muscle, their grace outshines any ballet dancer, and their resilience, akin to the ancient oak, withstands storm after storm. Their beauty - an amalgam of character depth, confident poise, and a style uniquely their own - leaves an indelible mark on the hearts of those fortunate enough to bask in their radiance.

Time, that elusive entity, for them, is a pearl of great price. It slips through the fingers like fine sand, forever flowing, eternally escaping. Yet, they understand its true value. A resource that, once spent, cannot be recovered. They recognize the world's tick-tock dance to the rhythm of the universal clock. Each beat, each second, is a priceless opportunity to mold the present, to shape the future.

Indeed, the ledger of time is a shared possession, each of us bequeathed an identical 24 hours each day. However, the privilege to luxuriate in free time or shoulder additional responsibilities skews this distribution. Amid this ceaseless march, these women appreciate the present moment as their exclusive canvas for action and creation.

Throughout the day, they weave a tapestry of rich relationships and meticulously honed skills. Time, the grand maestro, orchestrating connections that demand effort, devotion, patience, and skills that are only refined by the relentless grind of practice. For these women, the passage of time is a classroom, a place of growth, and a space for healing.

When twilight casts long shadows, these women, these Black queens, return home. Their hearts brimming with gratitude for each opportunity seized, each challenge met head-on, each moment lived with an unapologetic authenticity. Proud, resilient, and fierce, they wear their blackness as a crown, a testament to their indomitable spirit.

In this unwavering pride, in this celebration of self, they find the key to true freedom. Their whispers of affirmation echo through the night:

"I am strong. I am courageous. I am powerful. I am confident. I am free. I am a leader. I am a warrior. I am financially stable. I am indispensable. I am capable. I am me."

This book, dear reader, is a tribute to their spirit, a paean to their strength, an ode to the quintessential Black Queen. So, here's to you, women of the world, to those stepping out each day with heads held high, heels clicking in determination, crowns shining with purpose. It is your time to embrace your crown, own your influence, and walk in your power. Let your presence be so palpable that it ignites the world around you. Rise, shine, and claim your day. For you are the Essence of a Black Queen.

The Anatomy of a Queen

Beloved, I invite you on this journey of self-discovery, an exploration into the intricate architecture that forms the essence of a queen - you. Yes, you, who wear your grace as your crown, your strength as your scepter, and your resilience as your robe.

Let's step into the realm of Poise: The Importance of Grace in Leadership.

What does it mean to possess poise? It's an artistry of the spirit, an elegant balance that resides not just in your actions, but in your soul. Poise is the eye of the storm, calm and serene, even as life swirls around you. It's that soft voice in your heart that says, "I am enough. I am capable. I can weather any storm."

Grace, my dear, is your secret weapon. It is your calm in the face of chaos, your elegance in the midst of struggle, your resilience in the heart of adversity. It's the gentle sway of a willow tree standing tall against the mightiest of winds, whispering to the world that you will not be moved, that you will not be broken.

Leadership, you see, is not simply about wielding power or barking orders. It's about the gentle strength that radiates from your core, casting a soft glow that lights the path for those who look to you for guidance. Leadership is about embodying the grace that speaks volumes more than the loudest voice ever could.

This grace, this poise, is not something you need to seek in far-off lands or from other people. It resides within you, patiently waiting for you to reach inward and embrace it.

Do you feel it? That soft pulse of power coursing through you? That is your grace. That is your poise. That is your leadership.

The path to embracing this grace may not always be smooth. There will be times when the world will try to shake your foundation, to crack your calm exterior, to test your resilience. But remember, dear one, a diamond is formed under pressure, and so are you.

In these moments of pressure, I want you to close your eyes and imagine that soft, resilient willow tree. Feel the roots that reach deep within the earth, pulling strength from the soil. Imagine its sturdy trunk that does not break under pressure but sways with it, moving with the flow, bending but never breaking.

That is you.

That is your poise.

That is your grace.

That is your leadership.

And so, as we step forward on this journey, I implore you to hold onto your grace, to nurture your poise, to let your leadership shine. Your journey may be challenging, and at times, it may seem unending, but know this:

You are a queen.

You were born to lead, born to shine, born to be a beacon of light in this world. I know it. I believe in you. You will rise, you will shine, you will lead.

I see you, Queen. Embrace your grace, wear your poise, and let your leadership light up the world. You are the epitome of a resilient, graceful leader. And oh, how beautiful you are.

As Black women, we embody strength, grace, and resilience in all that we do. Our beauty extends far beyond physical appearance, encompassing a depth of character that is simply unparalleled. Whether it's the way we carry ourselves with poise and confidence, the way we present ourselves with impeccable style, or the energy and vitality that we bring to all of our endeavors, there's simply no mistaking the power of a Black woman.

Alongside these defining characteristics, Black women also understand the value and importance of time. Time is a resource that is often taken for granted, but it is one of the most precious things we have. Everything in the universe is bound to time, and its effects can be seen in the aging and eventual decay of all things. Time is intangible, and once it is gone, it is gone forever.

Despite the fact that everyone technically has 24 hours in a day, the amount of free time individuals have varies dramatically based on their privileges and responsibilities. No one knows how much time they have, and the present moment is the only space we have to work in. A person's perspective of the past and future can impact their happiness, and the way in which we manage our time can have a significant impact on our life.

Investing time in relationships and skills is crucial for personal growth and fulfillment. Relationships require a commitment of time and effort, and skills take time and practice to develop. Time serves as both a teacher and a healer, allowing us to grow and evolve.

This book is a celebration of the Black queen in all of us, and the unique qualities that make us who we are. It acknowledges the power and importance of time, and how it can shape and define our lives. The Black woman is a symbol of grace, strength, and resilience, and this book is a tribute to all that we are and all that we can be.

How to Showcase Your Strengths and Ideas Effectively

Hello, Beautiful. I see the strength that's shimmering within you. It's not just present, it's palpable. It's an energy that's eager to break free and shine a light on your unique gifts and incredible ideas. It's time for you to share these strengths with the world, and I want to help you do it with a presence that's as radiant as you are.

When you step into the world, whether it's into a boardroom, onto a stage, or into a room filled with loved ones, your presentation is your opportunity to put your best self forward. It's your chance to illuminate your talents and express your ideas effectively. This isn't just about what you say or how you look, but about the energy that you radiate - your very aura that paints a picture of who you are and what you're about.

Now, let me assure you, this isn't about pretending to be someone you're not. This isn't about perfection. It's about authenticity. It's about showcasing your natural strengths, those qualities that make you unique, those aspects that make you, you.

You might be thinking, "But Trenace', I'm not sure what my strengths are, or how to express my ideas effectively." That's okay, beautiful. This journey isn't about having all the answers. It's about discovery. It's about growth. It's about stepping into your power and knowing that you are enough, just as you are.

Let's begin by identifying your strengths. Look within. What are you passionate about? What ignites that fire within your soul? What are you naturally good at? What have others praised you for? These are your strengths. These are your gifts. Recognize them. Embrace them.

Now that we've identified your strengths, it's time to present them to the world. And this, my dear, is where your authentic voice comes into play. Your voice is more than just the words you speak - it's your ideas, your experiences, your wisdom. It's the story of who you are and what you believe in.

Your ideas are worthy. They are valuable. They are deserving of being heard. Express them with confidence. Express them with passion. Express them with grace. Know that when you speak from the heart, others will listen. They will connect with your authenticity, your sincerity, your truth.

When it comes to showcasing your strengths and ideas effectively, remember that you are not alone. You are surrounded by a sisterhood of queens, each one shining her unique light, just like you. Draw strength from this community. Learn from one another. Lift each other up.

So, step forward, my queen. Embrace your strengths. Share your ideas. Shine your light. Present yourself to the world with confidence, with grace, with authenticity.

I see your potential. I see your power. I see your light.

And oh, how it shines.

I believe in you, and I know that you will present your unique gifts and remarkable ideas to the world with grace and authenticity. Step into your brilliance. Step into your power. Step into your light. You were born to shine.

Harnessing Personal Energy for Productivity and Leadership

Queen, your energy is more than just an abstract concept. It's a force to be harnessed, a wellspring to be utilized, a sacred reservoir of strength and resilience that's distinctly yours. Knowing this, let's draw from our sisters who've brilliantly harnessed their energy, using it to blaze trails and redefine boundaries.

Firstly, consider Mellody Hobson, the powerhouse president of Ariel Investments and the chairwoman of Starbucks. Her secret? Understanding and managing her energy levels. Despite the long hours and myriad responsibilities, Mellody has always recognized the value of prioritizing self-care and health. Every day, no matter how packed her schedule, she ensures that she exercises and eats right. She understands that her physical health is directly linked to her energy levels, and consequently, her productivity.

On the research front, a significant study by Tony Schwartz and Catherine McCarthy titled "Manage Your Energy, Not Your Time," published in Harvard Business Review, proved that the key to increased productivity, healthier relationships, and more fulfilling lives lies in learning how to manage and renew our energy. They discovered that employees who took a break every 90 minutes had a 30% higher level of focus and a 50% greater capacity to think creatively.

Let's also look at Oprah Winfrey, the media executive, actress, talk show host, television producer, and philanthropist. Oprah's life stands as a testament to the power of energy management. From her disciplined morning routine of meditation and exercise to her conscious efforts to maintain positive relationships, she embodies the wisdom of focusing not just on the hours of the day but on the energy she brings to those hours.

Now, dear queen, let's translate these inspiring stories into action. Start with self-awareness. Begin to notice the ebb and flow of your energy throughout the day. Are you most productive in the morning or do you find your stride later in the day? Use this awareness to schedule your most demanding tasks during your peak energy periods.

Nurture your body. Your physical health is vital for maintaining high energy levels. Regular exercise, a balanced diet, adequate sleep - these are not luxuries but essentials. Just as important is your emotional health. Surround yourself with individuals who uplift and inspire you, those who fuel your energy rather than drain it.

Breaks aren't a waste of time, but a way to renew your energy. Whether it's a brief walk, some quiet meditation, or simply sitting with a cup of tea, take regular pauses to recharge and rejuvenate.

As you begin to harness your personal energy, you'll see a remarkable increase in your productivity and capacity to lead. Your energy, beautiful queen, is your secret weapon. Wield it wisely and see how it transforms your world. You are the master of your energy. Own it. Harness it. Unleash it. And in doing so, light up the world with your brilliance.

Embracing Your Crown

It's critical to realize that harnessing your energy is a dynamic process that involves purposeful action and constant reflection. In light of this, let's consider some actionable strategies that you can incorporate into your daily routines to help improve your time management skills, bolster your leadership abilities, and fortify your self-care practices.

1. Set Priorities: Clearly define what's important to you, both in your personal and professional life. As a Black woman, you're likely juggling multiple responsibilities, and setting priorities can help bring clarity and focus.

2. Embrace Self-Care: Remember, you cannot pour from an empty cup. It's essential to carve out time for self-care. This can take many forms, from exercising and eating well, to meditating, journaling, or simply spending time with loved ones.

3. Learn to Delegate: Whether in your personal life or your professional one, understand that you don't have to do everything alone. Where possible, delegate tasks to free up time and mental space.

4. Use Tools: Make use of digital tools and apps to manage your time and tasks more effectively. Tools like calendars, reminders, and project management apps can make a big difference.

5. Practice Mindfulness: Try to be present in the moment. This helps you to focus and can also lead to increased enjoyment and fulfillment in what you're doing.

6. Schedule Breaks: Just as you schedule your tasks, schedule regular breaks to rest and rejuvenate. Remember, breaks aren't a luxury, they're a necessity.

Now, queen, let's shift our gaze to a daily exercise that can foster your leadership skills and self-care practices. I call it the "Triple A Exercise": *Acknowledge, Appreciate, and Aspire.*

1. Acknowledge: At the end of each day, acknowledge one thing you did that you're proud of, no matter how small. This could be anything from a challenging task at work, a creative problem you solved, or a personal goal you reached.

2. Appreciate: Reflect on one thing about yourself that you appreciate. This could be a personal quality, a physical attribute, or a skill you possess.

3. Aspire: Finally, think of one goal or aspiration for the next day. This could be something you want to achieve, a challenge you want to tackle, or a task you want to complete.

By focusing on these three aspects – acknowledging your achievements, appreciating your unique qualities, and aspiring to continue growing –

you're nurturing a positive mindset, celebrating your progress, and setting the stage for continued growth and success.

Lastly, remember, beautiful queen, your journey to success is your own. It's okay to pause, to rest, and to move at your own pace. Your worth is not determined by your productivity, and you're not alone in your journey. Each step you take, no matter how small, is a victory in itself. Embrace your journey, harness your energy, and let your light shine. You're capable, powerful, and deserving of every dream that sparks in your mind.

The Delusion of Multitasking

Chapter 2

Alright, queen, now that I was super nice to you in the first chapter, it's time we got real about this whole idea of multitasking. Now, I know you're out there doing your best, juggling a million things at once, thinking you're getting ahead. But honey, it's time we unpack this delusion of multitasking. Yes, you heard me right - delusion. 'Cause truth be told, this supposed superpower might be doing more harm than good. You ready to dive in? Let's get into it.

Picture this: you're on a conference call, checking your emails, scrolling through your socials, and maybe even trying to help your child with their homework, all at the same time. You're feeling like a superhero, right? Well, think again. What you're actually doing is splitting your attention into tiny fractions, and not giving any one task the full attention it deserves. Let's be honest, that's not fair to you or the task at hand, is it?

Darling, your brain, amazing as it is, wasn't designed to handle multiple tasks simultaneously. Research has shown that when we try to multitask, our productivity drops by a whopping 40%. That's right, 40%! You're putting in double the effort but getting less than half the productivity. Doesn't seem like such a superpower now, does it?

And it doesn't stop there. Multitasking isn't just reducing your productivity; it's also increasing your stress levels. You know that feeling of overwhelm that creeps in when you're juggling too many balls in the air? Well, that's your body's way of telling you that it can't handle all the stress that comes with multitasking. And let's be honest, as queens, we got enough to deal with without adding unnecessary stress to the mix.

Now, I hear you, "But how am I supposed to get everything done?" Honey, the answer is simple: single-tasking. Focus on one thing at a time. Give it your all. Once you're done, move on to the next task. Not only will you get more done, but you'll also do it better. Plus, you'll find that you're less stressed and more satisfied.

Still not convinced? Let me drop some knowledge on you. A study by the University of London found that multitasking can drop your IQ by 15 points during cognitive tasks. That's similar to losing a night's sleep! Who in their right mind would willingly choose to lower their IQ? Not me and certainly not you, queen.

So, there it is, laid out plain and simple. Multitasking ain't all it's cracked up to be. It's time we ditched the cape and stopped trying to be superheroes. Let's be queens instead: wise, powerful, and capable of ruling our kingdoms one task at a time.

Now, take a moment, breathe, and think about how you can start single-tasking. Take it slow, one step at a time. Remember, it's not about doing it all; it's about doing what matters most, and doing it well. So put that multitasking myth to bed and start giving your tasks the royal attention they deserve. You've got this, queen!

Quality vs. Quantity: Focusing on the Right Tasks

Alright, my queen, time to sit down and have a little heart-to-heart about this idea of quantity versus quality. Now, I know we live in a hustle-hard culture that tells us to do more, achieve more, be more. But honey, let me tell you right now, that is one treadmill you don't want to be running on.

It's easy to fall into the trap of thinking that ticking off a gazillion tasks on your to-do list equals productivity. But let's spill the tea here: being busy and being productive are two entirely different things. It's like confusing a zirconia for a diamond. They might look similar, but one is priceless, and the other... well, not so much.

Let me break it down for you: It's not about how many tasks you're squeezing into your day; it's about what those tasks are and how well you're executing them. That's right, I said it - Quality over Quantity, darling!

Ever heard of the Pareto Principle, or the 80/20 rule? Well, if not, lean in closer, because this is some wisdom you need in your life. The principle says that 80% of your results come from 20% of your efforts. So, if you're focusing on the right tasks - the right 20% - you're going to see some powerful results.

Think about it. Is spending three hours perfecting a PowerPoint presentation really worth it when the rest of your tasks are crying out for attention? Sure, your slides might look fabulous, but what about that proposal you need to write, or that crucial client meeting you need to prepare for?

Now, I know it's hard, queen. As black women, we've been taught to do it all, to be it all. But here's the truth: doing it all isn't going to get you where you want to be. Focusing on the right tasks, the ones that move you closer to your goals, that's the secret sauce right there.

And let's not forget, doing fewer things allows us to do those things better. Instead of rushing through a task just to tick it off your list, take your time. Put in the effort. Make it shine. Because, let's face it, you're not just any woman; you're a queen. And everything a queen touches should be golden.

So let's switch things up. Instead of asking yourself, "How much can I get done today?" start asking, "What's the most valuable thing I can do today?" Prioritize tasks that align with your goals and offer the most significant rewards. And remember, sometimes less is more.

Embrace quality over quantity, and watch as your productivity skyrockets, your stress levels drop, and you start achieving your goals. And always remember, you're not just a busy bee, you're a queen bee. Rule your hive wisely.

Alright, now get out there and make me proud. Start focusing on what truly matters. Remember, you're not just juggling tasks, you're shaping your kingdom. Keep it quality, queen!

Reclaiming My Time: The Importance of Boundaries and Saying 'No'

Well, well, well, my queens! Today, we're getting down to the nitty-gritty, we're talking boundaries and the power of that tiny yet mighty word - 'No'. Yes, honey, I see that shudder, but don't fret, we're in this together.

So, let's start with a home truth, we all know that as Black women, we're often handed the short end of the stick. We are seen as the caretakers, the problem solvers, the doers, and the comforters. And you know what that does? It leaves little time for us to focus on ourselves, our dreams, our aspirations. But, baby, that stops today.

You see, your time is your kingdom, and just like any good ruler, you have to protect it fiercely. And that means setting boundaries. You might be wondering, "But how do I do that?" Girl, I'm so glad you asked.

Let's start with understanding that it's okay to put yourself first. Repeat after me, "My needs are important. My time is valuable." This ain't selfishness, darling. It's self-preservation.

Now, onto that powerful word, 'No.' It's a complete sentence, queen. You don't need to explain, justify, or apologize for saying 'No'. And let me let you in on a secret, most folks respect a person who can firmly, but kindly, assert their boundaries.

Remember that cousin who always asks you to babysit at the last minute or that coworker who's always trying to dump their work on you? It's time to stand up tall, look them in the eye, and with all the grace of the queen you are, say, 'No'. It might feel scary at first, but trust me, with practice, it gets easier.

Think about it, each time you say 'Yes' to something you don't want to do, you're saying 'No' to yourself. You're saying no to your peace of mind, to your dreams, to your growth. And baby, you deserve all of that and more.

Setting boundaries is all about respect - respect for yourself, your time, your energy. And when you start respecting your time, you'd be surprised at how quickly others follow suit.

So how about it, queen? Ready to reclaim your time? Ready to guard your castle against the time bandits and energy vampires? It's time to make yourself a priority. It's time to say 'No' to distractions and 'Yes' to your dreams.

Remember, there's a whole world out there waiting for you, and it starts by honoring your time and setting your boundaries.

So, put that crown on, straighten that spine, and step into your power. Because it's time to reclaim your time, your energy, your life. And darling, you're going to do it like the queen you are. Because you, my dear, are worth it. Now go out there and rule your kingdom!

Single-Tasking: Embracing the Power of Focus

Honey, let me talk to you real quick about this myth called multitasking. You know, it's that thing where you're supposed to juggle ten different things at once like you're in a circus act, right? Well, I'm here to tell you, that's not the way it's gotta be. Your brain isn't built for it. Fact is, it's single-tasking where the real magic happens.

You heard me, single-tasking. One thing at a time. Now, I know you're thinking, "But I've got so much to do!" I hear you, queen. We all got a lot on our plates. But let me ask you this: How well are you really doing those things when your attention is split across multiple tasks?

See, when we think we're multitasking, what we're really doing is task-switching. Our brain has to refocus each time we swap between tasks, and that takes time and energy. So, you may feel like you're getting a lot done, but, darling, you're likely just spinning your wheels. And you know what that leads to? Stress, mistakes, and that burnout feeling.

Instead, let's talk about embracing the power of focus. That's right, single-tasking is about honing in on one thing at a time, and it's a game changer.

When you focus on one thing at a time, you increase your productivity, you reduce your stress, and you enhance the quality of your work. Studies even show that people who practice single-tasking are more accurate in their work. Now, doesn't that sound nice?

How do you do it, you ask? Let me give you a few tips. First, clear away distractions. Yes, that means turning off those pop-up notifications on your phone and computer. Second, make a plan. Decide what you're going to focus on and then give it your undivided attention. Third, take breaks. Your brain needs time to rest and recharge. And finally, be patient with yourself. Changing habits takes time, but I promise you, it's worth it.

Now, I'm not saying it's going to be easy, honey. It's a discipline, and it takes practice. But I know you've got it in you. Remember, you're not just juggling tasks, you're juggling dreams. So give those dreams the focused attention they deserve. Because you, my dear, are not a circus act. You're a queen. And queens deserve to rule their time with focus and grace.

So, let's say it together, sisters: No more multitasking. Single-tasking is where it's at. One task, one focus. Now, let's get out there and show the world how it's done!

Time Batching: A Key to Efficient Work

Alright now, my fabulous queens, it's time to talk about something I know you're going to love. It's called time batching, and honey, let me tell you, it's about to take your productivity game to a whole new level.

So, what's time batching? It's not some newfangled kitchen gadget or fancy baking technique. It's a simple, but oh-so-smart, way of organizing your tasks to help you get more done in less time. It's about dedicating specific chunks of time to similar tasks. You know, like doing all your emailing at one time, or scheduling all your meetings back-to-back.

Now, why would you do this, you ask? Well, because, darlings, every time you switch tasks, your brain needs time to refocus. And that time adds up! By batching similar tasks together, you reduce the amount of task-switching you do, and that means you get more done. Simple as that.

But that's not all. Time batching also helps reduce distractions. Because when you know you've got two hours to write, and that's all you're going to do, you can put that phone on silent, close those extra tabs, and just get down to business. It's like a VIP party for your focus, and distractions ain't on the guest list.

Now, how do you start time batching? It's easy, honey. Just look at the tasks you do regularly, and see how you can group them together. Maybe you've got a lot of calls to make. Schedule them all in one morning.

Got a bunch of paperwork? Do it all in one go. You see where I'm going with this?

But remember, the key is to stick to your schedule. That means when it's email time, you're not checking social media or gossiping with your coworker. And when it's meeting time, you're not sneaking peeks at your inbox. Stay focused, my queens.

And one more thing: don't forget to schedule breaks. Your brain needs time to rest and recharge. So, make sure you're giving yourself time to breathe in between those batches.

Time batching ain't just about getting more done. It's about making your time work for you. It's about being efficient, reducing stress, and leaving more time for the things you love. It's about working smarter, not harder.

So, let's get batching, ladies! With a little bit of planning and a lot of focus, you'll be amazed at what you can achieve. Remember, you're the queen of your time. Now go out there and rule it with grace and efficiency.

The Art of Delegation: Empowering Others to Lighten Your Load

Alright, my royal divas, let's get real for a minute. We are some hardworking, do-it-all, powerhouses! We run businesses, raise children, keep homes, support friends, and often, we do all this without breaking a sweat. But here's the thing, ladies: just because we can do it all, doesn't mean we should. And that, my friends, is where the art of delegation comes into play.

Now, I know what you're thinking, "I can't just pass off my responsibilities to someone else!" And I hear you, sis. We've been conditioned to believe that we need to do it all ourselves. But let's break it down. Delegation is not about passing the buck or shirking responsibilities. It's about empowering others to share in the work, so you can focus on what you do best.

Think of it like this: a queen doesn't do all the work in her kingdom. No, she empowers her trusted advisors, her skilled craftspeople, her trained soldiers to do their jobs. She oversees, yes, but she doesn't do it all. And you shouldn't either.

Delegation is about knowing your strengths and the strengths of your team. It's about understanding that every task does not require your unique touch, and that there are tasks that others can do just as well, if not better than you can.

So how do you do it? First, you need to identify the tasks that can be delegated. Look at your to-do list. What tasks are taking up time but not necessarily utilizing your specific skills or talents? Those are prime candidates for delegation.

Next, match the task to the right person. Who on your team has the skills, the time, and the desire to take on this task? Once you've identified that person, have a conversation with them. Explain why you're delegating this task, what the expectations are, and how it fits into the larger goals.

And here's the hard part, my queens: Let it go. Once you've delegated, trust in the ability of your team to get the job done. Sure, there might be questions or issues that come up, but resist the urge to step in and take over. Provide guidance, yes, but remember, the point is to lighten your load, not to micromanage.

I know, it's easier said than done. Delegation can feel like you're losing control, or like you're piling work on others. But remember this: When you delegate, you're not just lightening your load. You're also empowering others, building trust, and strengthening your team.

In the end, queens, delegation is about recognizing that you are not alone. You have a team, a support system, a village. And with their help, there's nothing you can't achieve. Now that's some real queen behavior! So go ahead, give it a try. Delegate, and watch your kingdom flourish.

Your Energy Is A Precious Commodity

Alright, my queens, we've walked a journey through this chapter together, learning, growing, and hopefully, changing the way we think about our time. We've shined a light on the delusion of multitasking and discovered that, in reality, doing one thing at a time is where we truly shine.

We've uncovered the secret that it's not about doing more, but about doing the right things - quality over quantity, always. We've embraced the truth that boundaries are not barriers, but bridges to balanced living. By learning to say 'no' more often, we say 'yes' to our wellbeing, our dreams, and our true selves.

Remember, your energy is a precious commodity, beautiful queen. Don't scatter it on tasks that aren't serving you. Embrace the power of single-tasking. Turn your attention fully to one task at a time and watch as the quality of your work improves, your stress levels decrease, and your satisfaction soars.

And let's not forget about the magic of time batching. This ain't just about managing your hours, it's about owning them, controlling them, and bending them to your will. Bundle similar tasks together and give them a dedicated slot in your day. You'll be amazed at how your productivity spikes, and how the distractions fade away.

Finally, let's talk about that delegation, honey. You are a queen, not a martyr. There is no crown for the woman who does it all. Instead, there's a circle of trust and empowerment when we allow others to help carry the load. Remember, you are a leader, not a lone soldier. Delegate. Trust. Breathe.

So here's your call to action, my divine divas. Take these lessons, let them sink deep into your heart and your mind. Reflect on your own habits, your own beliefs about time and work. And then, take action. Make changes. Try single-tasking. Experiment with time batching. Practice saying 'no.' Delegate a task.

Above all, remember that this isn't about becoming someone else. It's about becoming the best version of you. The you who is in control of her time. The you who is focused and productive. The you who is not just surviving, but thriving.

Remember, my queens, you are powerful, you are deserving, and you are enough, just as you are. But you also have the power to grow, to change, and to become even more amazing. So take these tools, this wisdom, and use it. Not to build a wall around yourself, but a ladder. Climb it, queen. Reach for the stars. Your time is now. Shine on!

Reign Supreme — Becoming Your First Priority is Key

Chapter3

Alright, my queens, gather 'round now, because we're closing this chapter on a high note. This chapter's been all about one thing: you. 'Cause honey, it's high time we remember that, in the grand symphony of life, you are the melody. You reign supreme, not in the background, but at the very forefront.

Let's be real, putting ourselves first ain't as easy as they make it out to be. It feels like climbing a mountain in a hailstorm sometimes, especially post-2020. Our world has been shaken and stirred, and still, we find ourselves asking, "how can I possibly put myself first?" But let me tell you, my queens, that's where the magic happens. We need to remember that to help others, we need to help ourselves first. That's not selfish, that's survival.

It's about donning that oxygen mask of self-love and care before we can help anyone else breathe. It's about realizing that yes, rest is essential, not a luxury. It's about drawing boundaries, and while that might feel as foreign as speaking another language, it's vital. It's about understanding that, yes, I do deserve what I'm asking for. It's about taking that swimming upstream and turning it into a victory lap.

Queens, our hesitations often root from societal pressures, expectations, and norms. We're told to prioritize others, to equate hard work with zero rest, and that love means always saying 'yes.' But we're here to rewrite those rules, baby! You are worthy of prioritizing yourself, of saying 'no' when needed, and, most importantly, of unapologetically asserting your needs and desires.

Dr. Allan brings us a tool, a gem of a solution. Find that one person, your cheerleader, who can say, "You taking care of yourself is something I want for you." Build that community that supports your growth, that wants for you what you want for yourself. It's a powerful thing, my dears, to have a support system that helps you put yourself first.

This journey may feel like you're drawing a line in the sand, that by setting boundaries, you stand alone on one side while others resent you on the other. But here's the kicker: You ain't alone. Your cheerleader, your support system, stands by your side, lifting you up, reminding you that your needs and desires are valid, no matter what anyone else might say.

So, my beautiful queens, as we close this chapter, take these words to heart. Prioritize yourself, even when it feels like you're swimming against the current. Understand that it's okay to need a boost, to need a reminder that you are worthy. Reach out to your cheerleaders, let them remind you of your power, your worth, your light.

Remember, you are a queen, and you reign supreme. Take that bath, book that therapy session, splurge on that staycation, say 'no' when you need to. You're not just allowed, you're encouraged. You're not just worthy, you're deserving. Prioritize yourself, queen, and let the world adjust to your rhythm. Because you are worth it, you have always been worth it, and you will always be worth it. Shine on, my queens, shine on!

SELF's Guide to Caring for Your Mental Health

Now, we all know the past year and a half have tested us in ways we could never have imagined. We've seen things, we've felt things, and let's not beat around the bush - it's been rough. But here's the silver lining, the beacon of hope in the foggy night - we've learned to talk about our mental health. We've begun to lift the veil of stigma, piece by piece, and that, my queens, is progress.

But just talking ain't enough, honey. You can't fix a flat tire by just acknowledging it's flat. We've got to roll up our sleeves, get our hands dirty, and do the work. We've got to prioritize our mental health because, let's be real, if we don't, who will?

And that's where this guide comes in, my loves. It's your road map, your compass, your GPS on this journey of mental well-being. It's our way of saying, "we see you, we hear you, and we're here to help you." It's packed with tips, advice, and resources to guide you through the maze that is mental health. Whether you're seeking a therapist, exploring a new mental health technique, or just taking your first step on this journey, this guide is your trusted companion.

Remember, my queens, this is not a race, it's a journey. A journey towards better mental health, towards self-love, towards peace and resilience. And every step you take, no matter how small, is a victory. Every time you reach out for help, every time you take a break, every time you say, "I'm not okay," you're winning. You're choosing yourself, your health, your well-being, and there's nothing more powerful than that.

So, my beautiful sisters, as we wrap up this chapter, take this to heart. Prioritize your mental health, because you matter. Your feelings matter. Your well-being matters. Reach out for help when you need it, lean on your support system, embrace self-care. Use this guide as a tool, a stepping stone towards better mental health.

And remember, you are not alone in this. We are in this together, hand in hand, step by step. You are strong, you are capable, and you are worthy of happiness and peace. Let's lift each other up, let's support each other, let's break the chains of stigma together.

You are a queen, and your mental health matters. So, let's take care of it, let's nourish it, let's cherish it. Here's to our mental health, my queens. Because we're worth it, and we deserve to live our best lives, mentally, emotionally, and physically. Onward and upward, my queens, onward and upward!

The Unselfish Art of Prioritizing Yourself

Let's put some things straight here. We've come to the end of this chapter, and let me tell you, there's a whole lot of wisdom in these pages, but here's the final sermon for today: It's about time we get unapologetically selfish, because taking care of yourself, honey, is the best gift you can give to others and to the world.

Now, I know what you're thinking. Being selfish? But that ain't good. Well, my queens, let me redefine selfish for you. You see, prioritizing yourself isn't about neglecting others, it's about refueling, recharging, and reigniting your own spark so you can shine brighter for those around you. It's about embracing the art of self-love, self-care, and self-respect.

So, why should we prioritize ourselves, you ask?

First off, we've all heard the saying, "You can't pour from an empty cup," right? It's a simple truth. If we keep pushing and pushing ourselves for others, never taking time to replenish our energy, we'll end up depleted, burnt out, and having nothing left to give. It's not just us who suffer, but those around us too. Our kids, our partners, our friends, they all deserve the best of us, not what's left of us.

Secondly, doing what we love recharges us. When we take time for ourselves, indulge in what lights us up and brings us joy, we become radiant. We bring that joy and energy back into our interactions with others. You ever noticed how a mama's date night or a sister's spa day ends up benefiting everyone around them? That's the magic of self-care, my loves.

Thirdly, we lose ourselves when we're always on the go. When we're always in the hustle and bustle of the "do, do, do" mentality, we often forget who we are. We sacrifice our own interests, we neglect our passions, and in the process, we become strangers to ourselves. But honey, the world needs you, the real you, not the 'lost in the crowd' you.

Moreover, we can drain others when we neglect our own needs. We don't want to be that woman who leans too heavily on her children, her partner, her friends to fulfill her own needs. It's not fair to them, and it's not healthy for us. Instead, we should strive to be fully formed, fulfilled individuals who inspire others by our example.

Then there's that pesky "critical inner voice." This one's tricky, my sisters. It loves to make us feel guilty for taking time for ourselves, calls us selfish for prioritizing our own needs. But remember this, we are worthy of self-love and self-care. Don't let that voice tell you otherwise.

And lastly, neglecting ourselves leads to stress, and stress hurts us and those around us. It affects our mental and physical health, our relationships, and our overall wellbeing. And what good are we to others if we're always stressed and strained?

So, my queens, as we close this chapter, remember this: Prioritizing yourself isn't selfish, it's essential. It's the key to living a fulfilled, happy, and balanced life. Let's break these chains of guilt and start embracing self-love and self-care. We are queens, and we deserve to be treated as such, first and foremost by ourselves. So, let's put on our crowns, let's care for ourselves, let's prioritize ourselves. We owe it to ourselves and to the world.

Why It's So Hard For Queens To Prioritize Themselves

I ain't here to sugarcoat or smooth-talk things for you, but to lay down some cold hard truth. And the truth is, us black women are a force to be reckoned with, but we need to recognize our own worth before the world will follow suit. Now, I ain't saying it's easy, but I'm telling you it's necessary.

See, the world has conditioned us, trained us, and pushed us into this mindset where we're always putting ourselves last. From childhood, we're taught to take care of others, to be selfless and caring, and yes, that's an admirable trait. We've got hearts as big as the universe, but honey, you can't pour from an empty cup. It's high time we start thinking about ourselves, too.

I know what you're thinking, "That's selfish," right? Well, let me tell you something, sugar, self-care ain't selfish. It's survival. It's you taking control, it's you saying, "I am important too." This mentality, this Survivor Self as they call it, might have helped us cope in the past, but let's shed those old ways and begin to thrive.

Now, I ain't gonna lie to you, prioritizing yourself won't come easy. You're gonna have to learn to say "no" sometimes, and I know, I know, that ain't always easy. Guilt might creep up on you, guilt for not living up to this image of the superwoman we're supposed to be. But remember this, darling, you are a superwoman, but even superwomen need a break.

We've got to get to a point where we understand that the guilt is just noise, honey, and we need to tune into our own frequencies. When we filter out that guilt and focus on our true feelings, we can start living authentic lives that reflect our own desires and needs.

And you know what else? As you begin to prioritize yourself and pour into your own cup, your community will notice. They'll see the change, the glow, the energy. You'll be giving from a place of overflow, and trust me, that is a gift that keeps on giving.

I know it's a journey, and it's one that can feel lonesome at times. But darling, you ain't alone in this. We're all fighting similar battles. That's why it's essential to surround yourself with a tribe of women who are on the same path, women who understand the importance of self-prioritization.

Find your sisters, form your alliances, and lean on each other. Attend workshops, join groups, and participate in discussions where you can focus on yourself without the 'shoulds' of life breathing down your neck. It's about giving yourself permission, space, and time to just be, to just exist for you.

Now, remember this, my queens, you are radiant, you are fierce, and you are deserving of love, care, and attention, especially from yourself. So take a stand, reclaim your time, prioritize yourself, and watch as the world follows suit. You got this, ladies. Let's walk into our power, our health, and our well-being. It's our time now. You feel me? Good, now let's do this.

Establishing a Daily Routine for Optimal Queen-Time Management

it's time to discuss one of the most crucial aspects of self-care and self-love – establishing a daily routine for optimal queen-time management.

Now, let's get real for a moment. We juggle work, family, friends, passion projects, and the list goes on. And too often, we're falling into bed at night, exhausted and wondering where the heck our day went. But guess what? It doesn't have to be like that. You don't have to feel like a hamster on a wheel, just running, running, running and getting nowhere fast.

We can't add more hours to the day, but we can manage the hours we have more effectively. That starts with a daily routine that prioritizes YOU. Yes, my sisters, you heard me right. You, your well-being, your passions, your joy – all of that needs to be at the top of your to-do list.

First things first, start your day with gratitude and positivity. That's right, before you even roll out of bed, take a moment to give thanks for a new day and set a positive intention. This simple act can set the tone for your whole day.

Next, schedule in time for movement and nourishment. Whether it's a morning walk, a lunchtime yoga session, or an evening dance-off in your living room, find a way to move your body. Feed it wholesome, nutritious food that makes you feel good. This ain't about weight loss or looking a certain way – it's about taking care of your body because you love it, not because you're punishing it.

Then, we get to work. And when I say work, I don't just mean your 9-to-5. I mean your passions, your projects, your dreams. Don't put off your desires for "someday". Someday is now, my queens. Make time for what sets your soul on fire, even if it's just 15 minutes a day.

Now, don't forget to rest. I mean real rest, not just collapsing into bed after a long day. Schedule in time for relaxation and rejuvenation. Take a bubble bath, read a good book, meditate, or simply sit in silence. Your mind and body need time to recharge, so give them that.

Lastly, and perhaps most importantly, cultivate an attitude of self-love and kindness. We're often our own worst critics, but it's time to change that. Speak to yourself with love and respect. Treat yourself the way you would treat your best friend.

I know this all might seem like a lot to manage, but remember – Rome wasn't built in a day, and neither are life-changing routines. Take it one step at a time, and remember, it's okay to stumble. The important thing is to get back up and keep moving forward.

So, let's get started, ladies! Let's create daily routines that honor us, nurture us, and make us feel like the queens we truly are. I believe in you, and I know you can do it. Let's rise and shine, sisters! It's time to own our days and live life on our terms. Now go out there and show the world what you're made of!

If The Queen Isn't Well, The World Is Not Well

Listen up, queens, 'cause it's time to put a bow on this chapter with a vital message. As black women, we've been holding up the world since time began, taking care of everything and everybody, often at the expense of our own well-being. Now, I'm about to drop some truth. Hear me out, honey, 'cause this is vital: You can't pour from an empty cup. Until you're well, the world can't be well.

Don't get me twisted – this isn't about shirking your responsibilities or turning your back on your loved ones. No ma'am! This is about recognizing your worth and stepping into your power. This is about realizing that before you can give to others, you gotta give to yourself.

Let me tell you something, sister, you ain't no side dish. You are the main course, the pièce de résistance! You're not here to play small or shrink yourself to fit into someone else's box. You are here to shine, to soar, to be unapologetically you. And to do that, you've got to put yourself first.

I'm not talking about becoming a diva or a drama queen, although, honey, if that's your thing, you do you! I'm talking about taking care of your physical, emotional, and spiritual health. I'm talking about filling your own cup until it overflows.

We've got to rid ourselves of the notion that self-care is selfish. That's a lie we've been sold for too long, and it's time we cancel that subscription. Hear me now: taking care of yourself is the most selfless act you can perform. 'Cause when you're operating at your best, you've got so much more to give to those around you.

Now, I know what you're thinking. "That's all well and good, but I don't have time to take care of myself. I'm too busy taking care of everyone else." Well, honey, let me ask you this: If you don't have time to take care of yourself now, when will you? Tomorrow? Next week? Next year? 'Cause let me tell you, there's no better time than the present.

We've got to shift our mindset from "I don't have time" to "I make time." 'Cause let's face it, if Beyoncé – a world-class entertainer, businesswoman, and mama – can find time for self-care, so can we. We just have to make it a priority.

So, I challenge you, my queens. Let's take a stand. Let's break the chains of self-neglect and step into self-love. Let's put ourselves first, not out of selfishness, but out of a deep and abiding love for who we are and who we can become.

You are beautiful. You are powerful. You are deserving. Don't let anyone – including yourself – tell you otherwise. The world needs you, but it needs you at your best. And for that to happen, you need to take care of you.

So go forth, my queens, and conquer. Own your power, own your worth, and remember to always put your own oxygen mask on first. Because you can't pour from an empty cup. And the world needs what you've got to offer. Now, let's go show them what we're made of!

Embrace Now — The Presence of the Present

Chapter 4

Alright now, it's high time we had ourselves a good, honest talk about this very moment - right here, right now. That's right, sweethearts, we're taking a moment to embrace the power of the present.

You see, as black women, we're natural-born hustlers. We're always pushing, always striving, always looking ahead to that next goal, that next challenge. And don't get me wrong, that hustle is a beautiful thing. It's gotten us where we are, and it's gonna take us even further. But sometimes, honey, we get so caught up in that hustle, we forget to take a step back, breathe, and embrace the present.

Now, listen here, I'm not talking about shirking responsibilities or ignoring what's to come. No, no. I'm talking about finding balance. About recognizing that yes, while there's always another mountain to climb, it's crucial — vital even, to pause every once in a while, look around and take in the beauty of right now.

You ever hear that saying, "Stop and smell the roses?" Well, darlings, it's more than just a cute phrase on a motivational poster. It's a call to action, a reminder that this moment, right here, right now, is as important as any future we're hustling towards.

So how do we do this, you ask? Well, honey, we start by breathing. Yes, you heard me, breathing. Deep, slow breaths. Let them fill you up, let them ground you. Then take a look around. What do you see? What do you feel? What do you smell, taste, touch? That's life, baby, happening right now.

Next, we bring gratitude into the mix. Y'all ever notice how, when you start counting your blessings, you suddenly have a whole lot more of them? That's 'cause when you're thankful for what you've got, you open up space for even more goodness to flow into your life. So take a minute each day to be thankful for where you are and what you have.

Now, let's bring our focus back to self-care - 'cause that's what this is all about, right? When you take care of yourself, when you're kind to yourself, you're able to be more present. You're able to show up fully in each moment, instead of just going through the motions. And when you show up fully, my queens, that's when the magic happens.

So, I'm challenging y'all, right here, right now. Embrace this moment. It's yours, and it's precious. Stop waiting for "one day" or "some day". Stop putting off your happiness for when you reach some arbitrary goal. Be happy now. Be content now. Be grateful, hopeful, excited, and in love with life - right now.

And remember, my queens, we only get this one life. We don't have time to wait for tomorrow. All we've got is right here, right now. And it's time we start living like it.

So, let's take a deep breath, let's look around and let's appreciate the beauty of this moment. Because this is it, honey. This is life, happening right now. And it's a beautiful thing. So, let's go forth, embrace the now, and live our best lives, one moment at a time.

Let's Get Present: Tuning Into the Here and Now

Alright, my radiant sisters, pull up a chair, it's time we sat down and gabbed about a little thing called mindfulness. Now don't be rolling your eyes at me. I see you. I'm not talking about no hocus-pocus, sit-with-your-legs-crossed hum-a-lot-of-om's type of thing (unless that's your jam, then by all means). No, I'm talking about embracing this very moment.

You remember that wise old Beatle, George Harrison? He sang it right, "It's being here now that's important. There's no past and there's no future. Time is a very misleading thing..." Ain't that the truth? We're always fussing over yesterday, stressing about tomorrow, but what about right now? This moment, this breath, this heartbeat - they're all we've truly got.

So, why is being all tuned in to the present such a big deal? I'm gonna break it down for ya.

1. You Are NOT Your Thoughts: Look, honey, our minds can be messy places. We get all tangled up in thoughts and worries that we forget they're just that - thoughts. They're not us. By being present, we can watch those thoughts come and go without letting them boss us around.

2. Goodbye, Procrastination: When we're mindful, we stop obsessing over the size of the task ahead. Instead, we focus on the very step we're taking. One foot in front of the other, and before we know it, we've walked a mile.

3. No More Autopilot: How many times have we zoned out, going through the motions without truly living? When we're present, every moment is intentional, meaningful, and vibrant.

4. Gratitude Is A Given: Living in the now makes it easier to see all the blessings around us. That gratitude ain't just good for the soul, it's a booster shot for the mind too.

5. A Healthy Mind: Mindful folks are happier, more content, more at peace. And honey, we all deserve a bit of that peace.

6. Setting Boundaries: When we're present, we understand our worth and the value of our time. We're not here to be doormats or carry everyone else's burdens. It's time we set boundaries and learned to say no.

Now, I'm not saying it's easy. No, ma'am. It takes work. But aren't we worth that work? Isn't it time we put ourselves first? We're queens, after all, aren't we?

It's time we start embracing the present, living each moment fully, and giving ourselves the love, care, and attention we deserve. Because, as George said, all there is ever, is the now.

So, ladies, let's take on this challenge. Let's be present. Let's be mindful. Let's cherish each moment, each breath, each heartbeat. Let's be the queens we are, right here, right now.

Queen, Unshackle Yourself: Embracing the NOW

It's time we had a little heart-to-heart about the power of now. You see, there's a secret weapon we all possess but seldom use - living in the present moment. This ain't just about stopping to smell the roses, this is about taking back your power, reclaiming your life, and shaking off those chains of past and future that keep us tied down.

Now, let me get this straight, the past and the future have their places. They're chapters in our life story. But honey, the present is where the magic happens, it's the main stage. It's the space where we're able to pull the strings, to call the shots, to put our plans into action. When we dwell on past hurts or future worries, we're missing our moment. We're like a star missing her own show.

Focusing on the present allows us to tap into the deeper levels of ourselves, forming stronger bonds with the world around us. And trust me, darling, when you're fully present, you're in a position to appreciate and express gratitude for every tiny blessing. That's where fulfillment lies.

But, let's get real, life ain't all sunshine and rainbows. We face challenges, hit stumbling blocks, and sometimes, life just knocks us down. But living in the present gives us the strength to face these hurdles head-on, to bounce back stronger and wiser.

Let's chat about the past, shall we? It's a tricky thing, the past. It's like a heavy old trunk filled with memories, both sweet and bitter. Sometimes, we get so caught up in rummaging through that trunk that we forget about the world outside. Dwelling on past mistakes and hurts doesn't do us any good, sugar. All it does is cloud our vision and weigh down our hearts.

Remember this - you are NOT your past. You are not defined by what's already happened, but by what you choose to do right now. The past can be a teacher, not a jailer. Let it guide you, not define you. And those mistakes? They're nothing but lessons dressed up in disguise. Don't let them hold you back.

So, my lovely ladies, it's high time we unshackle ourselves from past regrets and future anxieties. Let's live in the NOW. Let's make each moment count. Because in this present moment, we find freedom, we find joy, we find our power.

Life is a beautiful dance, my dears. Don't spend it sitting on the sidelines, dwelling on what was or worrying about what will be. Get up, dust off those dancing shoes, and take your place in the spotlight. Embrace the now, embrace your power, and dance like the queen you truly are.

Girl, Unchain Your Heart: Mastering the Art of Now

Alright, my beautiful queens, it's time to start learning to let go of yesterday and not fret about tomorrow. Life's too short, and the present - the here and now - is where we ought to live.

First thing's first, understand this, we all stumble, and we all get a little mud on our dresses. Perfection is an illusion, darling. Let's replace those harsh self-judgments with some tender self-love. The scars and scratches? They're nothing more than proof that you've lived, you've learned, and you're stronger for it.

Now, let's talk about those chains from the past, those grudges and resentments that we all tend to hold onto. Baby girl, they're just heavy luggage that slows you down on your journey. Let's replace those grudges with forgiveness, let's exchange those resentments for understanding. It's about freeing yourself to move boldly into your bright future.

Practicing mindfulness can help bring you back to the present when your mind starts to wander down memory lane or race ahead to the unknown future. Meditate, journal, take a stroll, or simply breathe in deeply and exhale the stress out. The past is a place of reference, not residence. And the future, it's a land of plans, not fears.

Now, let's touch on the future. It's like standing at the edge of a vast ocean, isn't it? Endless, unknown, and a little scary. But fear not, darling, because you were made to sail, not to anchor at the shore. Worrying about what's on the horizon robs you of the joy that's right in front of you. It's like trying to run with your eyes fixed on the sky – you'll miss the beauty at your feet.

Having plans, setting goals - that's a good thing. It's like setting the sails for your voyage. But remember, plans are there to guide you, not to tie you down. Striking that balance between planning for the future and savoring the present is the key.

When the fear of the unknown threatens to steal your peace, focus on what you can control. You can't control the wind, but you can adjust your sails. Develop a growth mindset, embrace challenges, and remember that every storm brings a rainbow.

Incorporate mindfulness techniques into your daily routine to help keep you grounded in the now. Meditation, yoga, or even just a few moments of silence can be the anchor that keeps you steady amidst the waves of life.

And finally, my lovelies, remember the strength in unity. Surround yourself with people who lift you up, who encourage you, who remind you of your worth when you start to forget. We're stronger together, and there's no hurdle too high when we stand shoulder to shoulder.

So, beautiful queens, it's time to let go of the past, embrace the present, and step boldly into the future. You are stronger than you know, braver than you feel, and smarter than you think. Unchain your heart, lift up your head, and claim your crown. Because, honey, you were born to shine.

Girl, Grab Your Power: The Unstoppable Force of the Present Moment

Listen up, my queens, because it's about time we gather up all the strength and wisdom we've got and claim the gift that's ours to hold - the present moment. See, the present is like an open field, waiting for you to plant your seeds and cultivate your dreams. It's the space where you take the wheel of your life, make your decisions, and map out your own journey.

Here's the real deal: the present is where change springs forth. When you live in the here and now, you got the power to shape your life and the world around you. You see, in the present, you're not just surviving, honey, you're thriving.

Think of it like a flowing river. Now, if you try to hold onto the past, you're standing at the river's edge, trying to catch water as it slips through your fingers. But darling, if you step into the flow of the present, you can ride the current, let it guide you, and find your way forward.

And let's talk about the future, it's the same thing. If you're constantly squinting down the river, trying to predict every twist and turn, you're going to miss the beauty right here, right now. But when you're present, you navigate life with skill and grace, able to handle whatever comes your way.

Now, let's talk about a real-life example of someone who has mastered the art of living in the moment and soared because of it. The queen herself, Oprah Winfrey.

From a childhood of hardship to becoming a beacon of inspiration for millions, this woman's journey is a testament to the power of the present. With every setback, every obstacle, Oprah chose to stay grounded in the now. She used her experiences to fuel her journey, never letting the past or future distract her from her path.

On her talk show, Oprah didn't just host conversations, she made connections. She was present with every guest, every audience member, every moment. And in doing so, she created a space for real, raw, transformative dialogue.

But, my queens, it's not just about the stars who've shone brightly. There are countless unsung heroes living their lives in the power of the present. Single parents working tirelessly to provide, entrepreneurs manifesting their visions, everyday people making a real difference. They are proof that the present is a force to be reckoned with.

So, my beautiful, strong women, take inspiration from these stories. Remember, the present is your playground, your power, your potential. By living fully in the here and now, you can shape your life, overcome any challenge, and make your dreams come true. Darling, it's time to seize the moment, because this moment, right here, right now, is yours to own.

Darling, It's Your Time: Practical Gems for Living in the Now

Alright, my queens, now that we've seen the magic of living in the present, let's take it from inspiration to action. I've got some golden nuggets, practical tips to help you seize the power of the present and let your light shine bright.

1. Make friends with mindfulness: Honey, mindfulness ain't no fancy term, it's about being fully tuned in to your life. Whether you're meditating, breathing deep, or just pausing to soak in the sunset, it's all about living in the now. Make it a daily habit, like brushing your teeth, and watch your life transform.

2. Get serious about self-care: Now, I ain't just talking bubble baths and chocolate cake. I mean taking care of you, mind, body, and soul. Prioritize the things that fill you up, whether it's a workout, a healthy meal, a good book, or some quiet time. Remember, you can't pour from an empty cup, honey.

3. Break free from negativity: We all have those moments when our thoughts spiral down into the dumps, dwelling on the past or fretting about the future. When you catch yourself in that downward spiral, hit the brakes. Replace those thoughts with positive affirmations or redirect your attention to the task at hand. You've got the power to steer your thoughts, darling.

4. Set goals and make them happen: Dream big, but break those dreams down into achievable goals. Then, take one step at a time,

and before you know it, you'll be on top of that mountain. Celebrate your progress along the way because it's about the journey, not just the destination.

5. Surround yourself with positivity: You know what they say, 'you are the company you keep.' So, make sure your circle is full of folks who uplift, inspire, and support you. Cut ties with anyone who dims your shine. You've got enough to deal with without the naysayers.

Now, my beautiful ladies, remember this ain't a race, it's a journey. Some days you'll nail it, others you might stumble. That's okay. Progress, not perfection, is the goal. Every step you take, every moment you embrace, brings you closer to becoming the empowered, present-focused, unstoppable queen you are meant to be.

So, take a deep breath, plant your feet firmly on the ground, and declare with all your might, "I am here. I am present. I am ready to live my life to the fullest." Because darling, it's your time to shine. And believe me, when you embrace the power of the present, there's nothing you can't do.

Black Women: The Catalysts of Change in the Economic Landscape

Chapter 5

Alright, my dear sisters, let's cut straight to the chase. We've seen the facts, we've analyzed the figures, and I know you might be feeling a little overwhelmed by this point. We've delved deep into the economic state of our Black America, and the weight of responsibility that's sitting on our shoulders. But let me tell you something, we Black women, we're not just survivors, we are thrivers.

We've come a mighty long way, don't let anybody tell you different. We are doctors, lawyers, CEOs, educators, leaders... we are change-makers, and we've been making that change while still being the backbone of our families and communities. We've not only held our own but carved spaces where there were none. We've learned to turn obstacles into stepping stones. You hear what I'm saying? This ain't a time for worry, it's a time for action.

We've been playing this game of life on hard mode for far too long, haven't we? The disparities, the systemic inequalities, the racial wealth gap - they exist, ain't no denying it. And yes, they are steep mountains to climb, but listen here, we are mountain movers. We didn't come this far to only come this far. So, let's roll up our sleeves, adjust our crowns, and get to work.

The first step in making change? Knowledge. We've got to understand our current economic situation before we can overcome it. That means getting real with ourselves about where we are and where we want to be. Knowledge is power, honey, and it's time we wield that power with all the grace and strength we possess.

But let's remember, we aren't just individuals out here. We're a community. A sisterhood. When one of us rises, we all rise. So, let's uplift each other. Let's empower each other. Let's take our young ones by the hand and lead the way. Show them that they can be CEOs, entrepreneurs, and financial experts. Tell them they can build wealth and break these chains of financial inequality.

And I'm not just talking about financial literacy, important as it is. I'm talking about instilling a belief in our girls that they can do anything, be anything. Show them what a strong, empowered Black woman looks like. Show them the grace of our struggle and the power of our triumph.

Now, let me level with you, sisters. This road won't be easy. It's going to require some serious hustle. But hey, aren't we the masters of that? Aren't we the ones who make a way out of no way? We've got this. We're not just capable, we're more than capable. We're phenomenal.

So, let's make some moves, ladies. Let's change this narrative. We're not victims of our circumstances; we're architects of our future. Each day, with each decision, we have the power to shift our reality. Every step we take towards financial independence, every young mind we enlighten, every sister we lift up, brings us closer to breaking these economic chains.

Remember, it's not just about surviving; it's about thriving. It's about building wealth, not just for us, but for our children, and our children's children. It's about leaving a legacy.

So, rise up, my sisters, rise up. We've got this. We've got the resilience of our ancestors running through our veins and the power of sisterhood at our backs. We are Black women, and there's nothing -

absolutely nothing - that we can't do. Now, let's get to work and continue to shine as we always do, like the Queens we are!

Black Women: Igniting Economic Change and Empowering Communities

Alright, my beautiful sisters, it's time we have ourselves a real, soul-baring, truth-telling kind of conversation. And it's all about us - Black women - and the phenomenal economic power we wield. Hear me out now.

This here, 2021, it's a year of transition. Our America is on a seesaw, trying to bring our economy back to life in the midst of this pandemic, while grappling with the long overdue call for social justice. It's a tall order, but guess what? We've got a solution, an answer that's been right under their noses, honey, and it's time to spotlight it: It's us, Black women. We are the catalysts, the spark plugs that can kick-start this economic engine and also, uplift our communities.

Look at the stats. Who's out there in the workforce, hustling harder than anyone else? We are. Doesn't matter if we're single or married, kids or no kids, young or old, we Black women are out there, punching those clocks and turning those gears. But here's the kick, despite our hard work, we're still making less, a whole $226 less per week than your average American. Y'all, that's over $11,000 in a year!

And it ain't because we don't want those high-paying jobs, it's the giant roadblocks, the barriers born from a toxic mix of systemic racism and discrimination that have limited our progress. Only one Black woman CEO in a Fortune 500 company. Only 4% of us in management roles. Only 3% of us as doctors. This, my sisters, has got to change.

Now, this ain't just about us. It's about the economy too. The workforce is going to need a whole lot of new blood in the coming years. Health care, education, community services, and oh, don't even get me started on the STEM field. They all need us. And it ain't just a win for us; it's a win for the whole darn country. More diversity means more innovation and better financial performance. We bring a unique perspective, a new way of seeing and doing things that can only boost this economy.

It's simple, honey: Invest in us. Give us the opportunities, let us show you what we can do. We're not just workers; we're innovators, leaders, creators. The moment we start breaking through those barriers and reaching those high-paying positions, that's when we'll see real change.

But it's not just about the money. When we rise, we lift our communities with us. We invest in our homes, our neighborhoods, our people. Plus, every dollar we earn helps to close that massive wage gap between women and men.

So here's what we need, sisters: More opportunities, better representation, fair treatment. With all the chaos swirling around us, this is something we can do, something that can bring about real, lasting change. Can you imagine the difference it would make, not just for us, but for our families, our communities, the whole U.S. economy?

Don't let anybody tell you different, we are worth investing in. And this isn't just something they should do, it's something they need to do. Right here, right now. We've got the power, the potential, and the passion. We're ready to step up and take our rightful place in this economy. Are you with me, sisters? Let's rise, let's shine, and let's make this economy work for us!

Queens of the Corporate Jungle: Overcoming Workplace Woes

I've heard the stories and lived the experiences, and honey, I know it ain't always easy. From feeling unfairly judged and unsupported, to dealing with tokenism and lack of recognition, it feels like we're caught up in a storm, doesn't it?

But let me tell you something, sugar. We are not victims, we're survivors. And these struggles? They're just stepping stones on our path to greatness.

1. Rise above the judgement: Some folks might have higher expectations of us, or judge us more harshly. We can't control their thoughts or biases, but we can control our reactions. Be ambitious, show your brilliance, and remember, queens don't let others define their worth.

2. Forge your own support network: Sometimes, the support we need isn't given to us. That's when we have to build our own. Connect with like-minded individuals, mentor each other, uplift each other. Together, we can face any storm, honey.

3. Move past the token role: It's true that sometimes we're seen as tokens. But that's not our identity. We're here because we're qualified, talented, and capable. Let's shatter those token labels and show them who we truly are - unstoppable forces.

4. Demand your recognition: We work hard, and we deserve to be recognized for it. If you feel overlooked, don't just sit back. Speak up, shine your light, and let your achievements be known. You're not bragging, darling, you're just stating facts.

5. Be the change: So you're the only one in the room? Use it as an opportunity. Speak up, make your presence felt, and pave the way for other queens to follow. Remember, you're not alone - you're a trailblazer.

6. Claim your interactions with leadership: Don't wait for them to notice you. Be proactive, share your ideas, voice your concerns. Show them that your voice matters, that you have something valuable to contribute.

7. Address the micro-aggressions: They might seem small, but they build up. Don't let them slide. Address them politely but firmly, and educate those around you. Every small step counts towards creating a more inclusive workplace.

These struggles might be real, but so is our strength, our resilience, and our ability to rise above. Remember, my darlings, every queen faces challenges. But it's how we overcome them that makes us truly royal.

So square your shoulders, lift your chin, and step into the battlefield with your head held high. You are a queen of the corporate jungle. You have the power to overcome, to thrive, and to create the change you wish to see. Your crown has been bought and paid for. All you must do is wear it.

Bossing Up: Black Women Rising in the Pay Ranks

We've been up, down, and around the block on the challenges we face in the workforce. We've acknowledged the reality, now let's take a minute to step into our power. Because we ain't just survivors, baby, we're thrivers! Let's talk about advancing Black women into higher-paying positions.

1. Know your worth: Did you know we only earn 63 cents for every dollar a white man earns? Now that's a hard pill to swallow. But remember this, my loves: knowing our worth is the first step to claiming it. We're worth every cent and more, and it's high time the world recognized it.

2. Rise above the education bias: Some folks might think that our earnings are tied to our education. But honey, that's a fallacy. We are educated, we are qualified, and we're not letting anything hold us down. Our degrees are more than pieces of paper, they're testament to our will, our determination, our intelligence.

3. Embrace your hustle: Did you know that we, Black women, have the highest labor force participation rate of all women? That's right, we're showing up, putting in the work, and making things

happen. But it's time to make sure that our hustle pays off in a way that truly reflects our dedication.

4. Tackle the unemployment rate: Yes, our unemployment rate has been high, especially due to the pandemic. But remember, my queens, every setback is a setup for a comeback. This is our moment to rise, to innovate, to adapt. We're turning the tide, and we're doing it in style.

5. Celebrate Black motherhood: To all my Black moms out there, you're the real MVPs. You're juggling motherhood and work like a boss, and you're showing the world that Black moms can do it all. You are an inspiration, not just to your kids, but to all of us.

So what's the game plan, you ask? It's time to boss up, my loves. Let's continue to educate ourselves, advocate for better pay, and ensure we're getting the recognition we deserve. Let's network, negotiate, and navigate our way to higher-paying positions. It's not just about closing the wage gap; it's about taking our rightful place in the hierarchy.

We've got the skills, the smarts, and the strength to rise above these disparities. And trust me, we will. We've got a legacy of resilience running through our veins, and we're not about to let a few obstacles stop us. We're climbing that corporate ladder, and we're doing it in our stilettos.

Now is the time to step into your power, my queens. Demand the pay you deserve, claim the positions you've earned, and shine your light bright for all to see. It's time for Black women to boss up and take the labor force by storm.

Remember, your worth is not defined by your wage, but your wage should reflect your worth. So hold your head high, know your worth, and don't settle for less. Because you're not just a queen, you're a boss. Now go out there and show them what you're made of!

The Triumph of Tenacity: Unleashing the Economic Potential of Black Women

Honey, let's wind this chapter up with some fiery truth and the kind of motivation that gets your blood pumping. Now, we've been through some heavy stuff in this chapter, but I'm here to tell you, it's all leading to something spectacular.

The McKinsey report, y'all remember that? It showed us the hard truth about where we are economically. Our challenges in the workforce, the barriers we face in climbing that corporate ladder - yes, it's all real. But you know what else is real? Our resilience, our determination, and our potential. Let's not forget, we are descendants of queens. Our history is filled with stories of Black women who've turned every stumbling block into a stepping-stone. And honey, we're about to do the same.

You see, we are not just workers, we are creators, innovators, leaders. Our economic power doesn't just lie in our ability to work, but in our ability to change the game. When we step into higher-paying positions, we don't just fill a gap, we create a ripple effect. We bring fresh ideas, new perspectives, a different kind of leadership that enriches the whole darn place.

And let's not forget the role we play in our communities. When a Black woman rises, she lifts her family, her neighborhood, her community along with her. Every dollar we make doesn't just benefit us, it uplifts all those around us. Now isn't that a powerful thing?

But sisters, here's the catch: We can't just wait for change to come knocking at our doors. We need to grab it by the collar and drag it in. This ain't the time for passive waiting, it's the time for active demanding. We need to step up, speak out, and claim what's rightfully ours. Higher-paying jobs? We deserve them. Better representation? We demand it. Fair treatment? We won't settle for anything less.

So let's get into action mode, my sisters. Let's arm ourselves with knowledge, build our networks, and sharpen our negotiation skills. Let's break through those glass ceilings and claim our place in the sun. And while we're at it, let's bring our sisters along. Because when one of us rises, we all rise.

And don't you dare listen to the voices that say you can't, because honey, you can and you will. Let's remember the words of our sister, Michelle Obama, "There's no limit to what we, as women, can accomplish." And we're about to prove that, aren't we?

Let this chapter not just be a reading, but a rallying cry. A call to every Black woman to tap into her immense economic potential and to redefine her destiny. Because we are not just survivors, we are thrivers. We're not just workers, we're changemakers. We're not just individuals, we're a powerful collective force.

So here's to us, Black women - the builders of economies, the nurturers of communities, the change agents of the world. Let's own our power, let's claim our worth, and let's ignite the change we wish to see. Because honey, we're just getting started. So, are you with me, sisters? Let's do this!

Caring for Self, Nourishing the Soul: Why Radical Self-Care is a Must for Black Women

Chapter 6

This chapter is all about you - your strength, your beauty, and your magic. But honey, there's one more thing we need to talk about, and that's radical self-care. I'm not talking about the occasional spa day or treating yourself to a new pair of shoes - although those are definitely part of it. I'm talking about a deep, soulful kind of self-care that nourishes your spirit, your body, and your mind.

Now, let's be honest. We, Black women, have always been the caregivers. We nurture our children, we support our families, we uplift our communities. We're often the first to rise and the last to rest. But my beautiful sisters, who takes care of us? Who nurtures us when we're weary, supports us when we're struggling, uplifts us when we're down? The answer, my darlings, is us. We are the ones we've been waiting for.

Let's not sugarcoat it - being a Black woman in this world ain't always easy. We face unique challenges and carry heavy burdens. We're dealing with systemic racism, bias in the workplace, health disparities, and the weight of expectations. Sometimes, it feels like the world is asking too much of us. That's where radical self-care comes in.

Radical self-care is about saying "enough" to the world's demands and saying "yes" to our own needs. It's about putting ourselves first, not as an act of selfishness, but as an act of survival. It's about acknowledging that we are worthy of care, of rest, of joy.

You see, my loves, radical self-care isn't a luxury - it's a necessity. It's as essential as the air we breathe, the food we eat, the water we drink. Without it, we cannot thrive. Without it, we cannot fulfill our true potential. Without it, we cannot be the phenomenal women we were born to be.

Radical self-care is about creating space in our lives for rest and rejuvenation. It's about honoring our bodies with nutritious food, regular exercise, and quality sleep. It's about nurturing our minds with positive thoughts, uplifting conversations, and continuous learning. It's about feeding our souls with love, joy, and inner peace. It's about setting boundaries, saying no when we need to, and protecting our energy.

But my darlings, here's the most beautiful part: When we practice radical self-care, we're not just taking care of ourselves. We're setting an example for our daughters, our nieces, our sisters. We're showing them that it's okay to put themselves first. We're teaching them that their worth is not tied to how much they do for others but to who they are - radiant, resilient, remarkable Black women.

So, my queens, here's my challenge to you: Embrace radical self-care. Treat yourself like the queen you are. Nourish your body, nurture your mind, feed your soul. You deserve it. You are worthy of it.

Remember, when you take care of yourself, you're not just sustaining your well-being; you're also igniting a revolution. A revolution where Black women are seen, heard, and valued. A revolution where we step into our power, claim our worth, and shape our destiny.

Now, are you with me, sisters? Are you ready to embrace this radical act of self-love and self-care? Let's do it, my queens. Let's care for ourselves with the same passion and commitment we give to others. Let's rise, let's shine, and let's flourish - for ourselves, for our communities, for our world. Because we, my darlings, are worth it.

Revolutionizing Self-Love: The Empowering Journey of Black Women

Now, my dearest sisters, we've been through a journey in this chapter, diving into the true depths of radical self-care. I know we've touched on some real truths, but hold on, 'cause there's still a word to be spoken. Let's get into it.

When we talk about self-care, we don't just mean taking a little time off. We're talking about a profound shift in the way we value ourselves. A revolution, if you will. We're talking about challenging the systems that have told us we're not worth it and proving them wrong. Because you best believe, we are worth it. Every single one of us.

Now, when you hear the word 'revolution,' you might think of protests, of fighting, of struggle. But remember, my queens, revolutions also come from within. We gotta rise up against the internal voices that whisper, "You're not enough." Those voices are lying, honey, and it's time to drown them out with the truth - you are enough, just as you are.

Radical self-care is about more than just taking care of ourselves; it's about revolutionizing the way we see ourselves. It's about claiming our worth and stepping into our power. And no one, my loves, can do that for us. We gotta do it for ourselves.

Think of radical self-care as your personal revolution. It's your declaration that you are important, that you matter. It's about giving yourself the love and respect you've been giving to everyone else. It's about saying, "I am a Black woman, and I am deserving of every good thing this world has to offer."

Now, this ain't a walk in the park, darlings. This journey will demand courage. But I know you have that courage. You have the courage to make choices that celebrate you, that affirm you. You have the courage to stand in your truth, your strength, your brilliance.

There's a world out there that's trying to tell you to dim your light, to make yourself smaller. But radical self-care is about rejecting that narrative. It's about shouting from the rooftops, "I am here, I am worthy, and I will not be ignored."

So, let's take this journey together, sisters. Let's boldly step into a future where we care for ourselves as fiercely as we care for others. Let's create a world where every Black woman knows her worth and isn't afraid to claim it.

This is your moment, queens. This is your time to rise. You have everything you need inside of you. You have the strength of your ancestors, the wisdom of your experiences, and the power of your potential. Embrace it. Celebrate it. Live it.

So, let's wrap this chapter up with a commitment, my beauties. Promise yourself today that you will embark on this journey of radical self-care. That you'll embrace this revolution of self-love. Make a vow to be your own best friend, your own biggest fan, your own shining light.

You've got this, my loves. I believe in you, and it's time for you to believe in yourself. So, let's rise up, let's shine bright, and let's show the world just how powerful we are. Remember, we are worth it - and don't let anyone tell you otherwise.

Awakening Your Inner Queen: The Radical Self-Care Revolution

Now it's time to wrap it up, not with a pretty bow, but with a spark of fire - a spark to light your path toward a healthier, happier, more balanced you.

Now, you may be asking, "What's this radical self-care?" So, let me break it down for you. This ain't about no pedicures or spa days - not that there's anything wrong with a little pampering, honey. But radical self-care? It's deeper. It's about taking care of your mind, your body, and your soul, in ways that respect and value the strong, gorgeous Black woman you are.

Physical wellness? Yes, indeed! I'm talking about fueling your body with the foods that nourish you, moving in ways that make you feel powerful and alive, and resting when your body tells you it's time. And trust me, if you're anything like me, that body will tell you!

Emotional wellness? You betcha! Let's face it, we all have those moments when we're feeling a little low. That's normal, my loves. But with radical self-care, you learn to navigate those emotions, to feel them, process them, and let them go. You learn to replace negative self-talk with self-love, self-doubt with self-confidence.

Spiritual wellness? Absolutely! This is all about connecting with your inner self and the greater power you believe in. It's about filling your spirit with love, peace, and joy. Whether you find that through prayer, meditation, nature, or something else entirely, it's all about feeding your soul.

Now, let me be real with you, my sisters. This ain't an easy road. It requires work. It demands that you push aside society's expectations and focus on your own needs. It asks you to prioritize yourself - and that can feel uncomfortable, especially when we've been taught to always put others first.

But here's the thing, queens. You can't pour from an empty cup. You've got to fill yourself up first. You've got to take care of you, so you can take care of the others in your life.

So, here's my challenge for you: Make radical self-care your daily practice. Treat yourself with kindness, compassion, and respect every day. Prioritize your needs, set boundaries, and say no when you need to. And, most importantly, know that you're worth it.

In this journey, you're not alone. You've got a sisterhood behind you, cheering you on, ready to catch you if you stumble. So, put on that crown, queen, and step into your power. You're stronger than you think, more beautiful than you know, and capable of more than you can imagine.

Remember, my loves, you're not just a woman; you're a force. You're a queen. And you deserve to be treated as such - by others, and by yourself. So let's get out there, embrace our power, and start this radical self-care revolution. Because we're not just surviving, darlings, we're thriving!

So, take a deep breath, put that smile on your face, and let's march forward into this new era of radical self-care. Are you with me, my sisters?

Because we are stepping into a revolution of love, strength, and resilience. And it starts right here, right now, with you.

Living Out Loud: Your Everyday Guide to Radical Self-Care"

We've explored the physical, the emotional, the spiritual. But now, honey, it's time to get down to the nitty-gritty. How do we live this radical self-care every day? How do we make it as natural as our morning coffee or our nightly skincare routine? Well, sit tight, my queens, 'cause I'm about to serve up some truths.

First and foremost, we need to rethink what 'care' means. This ain't about those moments of escape, those trips to the spa, or binge-watching your favorite show - though, trust me, there's a place for those too. No, this is about creating a life you don't need to escape from, one where self-care is just as routine as brushing your teeth.

.Start with your body, queens. Make healthy eating and exercise not something you do, but who you are. Get up, stretch out that gorgeous body of yours, move it in ways that feel good. And nourish it with foods that make you feel vibrant and alive. Remember, your body is a temple, so treat it with the respect it deserves.

Then, let's talk about your mind. Fill it with positive thoughts, surround yourself with people who lift you up, not drag you down. Make time each day for something that brings you joy - reading a book, listening to your favorite music, or simply sitting in silence and breathing deeply.

Spiritual wellness is up next. Find a practice that resonates with you, whether it's prayer, meditation, yoga, or even a quiet walk in nature. Make it a daily ritual, a time to connect with your inner self and the universe around you.

Now, let's get real for a moment, ladies. Radical self-care means setting boundaries too. You can't be everything to everyone all the time. Learn to say no without feeling guilty. It's not selfish, it's essential. Protect your peace, guard your energy, and prioritize your well-being.

Lastly, remember to celebrate yourself. Each day, find something you did well and give yourself a pat on the back. Remember, self-love is not vanity, it's sanity.

Now, my beautiful queens, none of this happens overnight. It's a journey, a daily commitment to yourself. And yes, there will be days when you stumble, when you don't quite meet your own expectations. But that's okay. This ain't about perfection; it's about progress.

Every day is a new opportunity to choose you. To prioritize your needs. To honor your body, mind, and spirit. To live out loud in radical self-care.

So, are you ready, my sisters? Ready to wake up each day and choose you? Ready to incorporate radical self-care into your daily life? Because I believe in you. I believe in your strength, your resilience, your power. And together, we can start this revolution of radical self-care, one day, one queen at a time.

Remember, queens, you are worth every moment of self-care you give yourself. You are worthy of love, of joy, of peace. So let's embrace this radical self-care, not just as an idea, but as a lifestyle. Let's do this, sisters. Let's make every day a radical act of self-love and self-care. Because we are worth it. Because we deserve it. And because, quite simply, we are amazing.

Shedding the Guilt: Embrace Self-Care and Self-Love with Open Arms"

There's one more mountain we need to conquer - guilt. That gnawing feeling that creeps up when we choose ourselves over others, when we put our needs first, when we dare to love and care for ourselves. Well, my queens, it's time to cast off those chains of guilt and embrace self-love and self-care without remorse. Are you with me?

First off, let's get one thing straight, sisters. Self-care is not selfish, and self-love is not vanity. These are acts of survival, acts of affirmation. We've been conditioned to believe that our worth lies in our sacrifices, in how much we can do for others. But I'm here to tell you, darlings, that's a lie.

Our worth is inherent, it's unchanging, it's rooted in who we are, not what we do. When we care for ourselves, when we love ourselves, we are affirming our worth, our value, our existence. And there's no guilt in that, my queens.

So, how do we shed this guilt? How do we embrace self-care and self-love with open arms? It starts with understanding. Understanding that we are human beings, not human doings. That we have needs and desires just like anyone else. And that fulfilling those needs, pursuing those desires, is not an act of selfishness but an act of self-preservation.

Next, we practice. Yes, my queens, shedding guilt is a practice, much like self-care itself. It's a daily commitment to choose ourselves without remorse. To say "yes" to our needs, our desires, our dreams. To prioritize our well-being over others' expectations. And each time guilt tries to creep in, we remind ourselves - I am worthy. I am deserving. I am enough.

Finally, we surround ourselves with support. Connect with your sisters who understand, who uplift, who inspire. Talk about your journey, share your struggles, celebrate your victories. Together, we can help each other shed the guilt and embrace self-love and self-care with open arms.

Remember, my beautiful queens, self-care is an act of love - for ourselves, for our bodies, for our minds, for our spirits. And love, my darlings, should never be shrouded in guilt.

So, let's make a pact, my sisters. Let's pledge to shed the guilt, to choose ourselves without remorse, to love and care for ourselves with open arms. Are you with me?

Let's do it, my queens. Let's rewrite the narrative. Let's create a world where Black women can care for themselves, love themselves, without feeling guilty. A world where our worth is recognized, our needs are prioritized, our existence is celebrated.

Remember, when you care for yourself, when you love yourself, you're not just affirming your worth, you're starting a revolution. A revolution of self-love, self-care, and self-acceptance. A revolution that begins with you.

Ready to shed the guilt, to embrace self-care and self-love with open arms? Because I believe in you, I stand with you, and together, we can conquer anything. Let's do it, my sisters. Let's start this revolution of radical self-care and self-love, guilt-free. Because we, my darlings, are worth it.

Straight Talk, No Chaser: Letting Go of Guilt and Embracing Your Power

Let's face it, we all mess up. Whether it's a harsh word said in anger, a promise we didn't keep, or not being there for a friend in need. We've all been there, done that, and got the guilt-filled T-shirt. Guilt, though, is a tricky beast. It hides in our minds and can sneak up on us when we least expect it, fueling that nagging voice that says we're not good enough, not doing enough.

We're all familiar with that lingering feeling of regret, the "I should've done this" or "I could've done that better". That's natural guilt, and it's normal. It's your moral compass saying, "Hey, maybe next time let's do things differently." But then there's chronic guilt, the kind that comes from being stressed out and overworked, feeling like you're never doing enough. Sisters, let me tell you, that kind of guilt isn't just unhealthy, it's unnecessary.

We have to remember, guilt isn't always about something we did. Sometimes, it's about something we didn't do, couldn't do, or had no control over. Feeling guilty for surviving a trauma when others didn't, or for being successful when others aren't, is called survivor's guilt. It's real, and it's tough, but remember this, honey: you didn't ask for those circumstances, and you can't control them.

And don't even get me started on that collective guilt, the type where you feel responsible for all the problems in your community, your city, or even the world! Baby, that's a heavy burden, and one you were never meant to carry alone.

Now, you might ask, "But how do I know if what I'm feeling is guilt?" Well, are you constantly criticizing yourself? Do you feel like you need to fix everything? Are you lying awake at night, worried about things you did or didn't do? If the answer to any of those is yes, that guilt is knocking at your door.

The Queen's Treasury: Financial Literacy and Empowerment

Chapter 7

Alright, my Queens, we've been through a lot. We've been breaking down barriers, shattering glass ceilings, and we've been doing it all with grace, style, and a whole lot of sisterly love. But now, let's chat about something a little different, something that's often overlooked but oh-so important for us to thrive: our financial health.

I know, I know. Money talks can be a bit, well, dry. But let me tell you something, ladies: understanding your money is like understanding the secret language of freedom, power, and opportunity. Let me say it louder for the ladies in the back: Financial Literacy is your ticket to the kingdom, your key to the castle!

Our coins, our cash, our hard-earned dough—it's more than just the means to pay the bills. It's about having the freedom to make choices, the power to shape our own lives, and the capacity to create a legacy for our children and our children's children. Yes, ma'am, your money is your voice, and your financial health is your strength.

Now, I don't want you to fret or feel overwhelmed. We've got this. We are queens, after all. So we'll start with the basics—budgeting, investing, and saving—and we'll break them down to be as easy as ABC. We'll walk through financial jargon, demystify it, and turn it into our own secret language of power and independence.

And then? Then we move to the next level. We'll talk about building empires, about investing in assets—not those fancy shoes or that chic bag, but real assets like property and businesses. We'll delve into entrepreneurship and see how it can be a path to wealth creation. And let's not forget about those all-important savings and emergency funds. Think of them as your financial security blankets, always there to keep you safe and warm.

Listen, my queens, our journey to financial literacy and empowerment won't be easy. We'll stumble, we'll face hurdles, but we will get back up. We will keep going because that's who we are. We're fighters, we're survivors, and we're queens. We'll take our hard-earned knowledge, our growing financial prowess, and we'll change not just our lives, but the lives of our families, our communities, and, yes, the world.

So, take a moment. Take a deep breath. And then, let's get ready to dive into this journey together. Let's arm ourselves with knowledge, power, and an unwavering commitment to our financial health. We're in this together, my queens. And remember, you've got this, and we've got you.

Because when a queen gets her coins right, she doesn't just build a castle. She builds an empire. And that, my dear queens, is a power play worth striving for. Here's to embracing our crowns and securing our financial futures!

Stable Thrones, Stable Queens: It's Time to Get Financially Literate, Sis!

Lean in and listen up because we're about to get real. We've all been there - bills piling up, bank account looking a bit thin, feeling like we're just scraping by. And why is it, honey, that it always seems like there's more month than money? But here's the deal: it doesn't have to be this way. And it starts with two words: Financial Literacy.

I can hear you now, "What's so important about Financial Literacy, sis?" Well, let me break it down for you. Financial literacy is about understanding money - how to make it, how to save it, how to grow it. It's about knowing your numbers, being intentional about your spending, and making your money work for you. It's about building a throne that's not just glittering in gold, but one that's solid and stable.

I won't lie to you, my queens, it's not going to be a cakewalk. It's gonna take time, commitment, and a willingness to learn. But I promise you, it'll be worth it. And here's why: when you're financially literate, you have the power. The power to make informed decisions. The power to create wealth. The power to break free from the shackles of financial insecurity and step into a future of financial freedom.

And this isn't just about you, my queens. No, no. When we become financially literate, we can pass that knowledge on. To our children. To our sisters. To our community. We can build a legacy of financial independence and prosperity. We can break the cycle of financial hardship that's been holding us back.

So let's start our journey, my queens. Let's arm ourselves with the tools and the knowledge we need to take control of our financial future. Let's learn to budget, to save, to invest. Let's learn to see our money not as something to be feared, but as something to be embraced. Because our money is our power, and when we have power, we have the ability to create change.

And when things get tough, and they will, remember this: you are a queen. You were born for greatness. You have the strength, the resilience, the courage to overcome any obstacle that stands in your way. You have the ability to learn, to grow, to succeed. And you are not alone. We're in this together, my queens, every step of the way.

Remember, my queens, a stable throne is built one brick at a time. So, let's start laying our bricks. Let's start building our stable thrones. And let's rise, my queens, let's rise to the heights of financial freedom, power, and prosperity. Here's to our journey, here's to our success, and here's to us, my queens. We got this!

Money Matters, Honey: Budgeting, Investing, and Saving Your Way to the Top!

We're talking budgeting, investing, and saving – the Big Three. Now, don't go rolling your eyes just yet. I know it sounds like the most boring trio since sliced bread, but hear me out. These three musketeers of money management have the power to take you from 'just making ends meet' to 'making money moves.' Are you ready to get this show on the road? I thought so!

First things first, let's talk budgeting. Now, I know that word can seem like a sour lemon that makes your face pucker, but it's time to squeeze that lemon and make some sweet, sweet financial lemonade. A budget is just a plan for your money, a blueprint for building your financial castle. It's about knowing where every penny goes and making sure you're spending less than you earn. It's about having enough for the essentials, setting something aside for a rainy day, and still having a little to treat yourself. You work hard, honey, you deserve it! Remember, a queen counts her coins and makes her coins count.

Now, onto saving. It's no secret that we black women are the backbone of our families and communities. We take care of everyone else, often at the expense of our own needs. It's time to flip the script and start prioritizing our financial health. Think of saving as taking care of your future self. That nest egg isn't just a safety net; it's a launch pad to help you reach your goals. Want to start a business? Buy a house? Travel the world? A solid savings plan can get you there. Start small if you need to, but start. Every little bit counts.

Finally, investing – now that's where the real magic happens. Investing is about growing your wealth, not just preserving it. It's about putting your money to work so that it can make more money. Sounds good, right? Now, I won't sugarcoat it; investing can be complex and risky, but with knowledge and guidance, it can be a powerful tool for financial growth. Learn about stocks, bonds, real estate, mutual funds – knowledge is power, my queens!

Remember this: Budgeting shows you where you are, saving determines where you can go, and investing dictates how quickly you get there. They are the trifecta of financial literacy, the keys to unlocking your financial freedom.

The journey to financial literacy won't be easy, my queens, but nothing worth having ever is. It'll take time, patience, and dedication. There'll be setbacks, sure, but remember, a queen knows how to rise after falling. Stay the course. Believe in yourself. You got this!

So, let's get our coins in order, my queens! Let's build budgets that work for us, start saving for our dreams, and learn how to grow our wealth. We are powerful, we are capable, and we deserve every bit of financial success. Let's make our money matter!

Financial Freedom: Unlocking Doors, Breaking Chains!

My Queens, it's time we discuss the crown jewel of financial literacy: freedom. Now, we aren't talking about the freedom to buy that designer bag you've been eyeing (although that's nice too!). No, we're talking about real, life-altering freedom and opportunities that financial literacy brings.

Wealth, my darlings, isn't about the size of your wallet. It's about the breadth of your options and the depth of your peace. So, let's get real about what financial literacy can do for you.

Financial literacy is like a map to your own personal kingdom. It's an escape route from the paycheck-to-paycheck hamster wheel, leading to a place where your money works for you. It's waking up in the morning knowing you're not a slave to your bills, but a master of your destiny. Imagine a life where the mailbox isn't a minefield of overdue notices, but a landing pad for opportunity. That's what financial literacy can do!

Being financially literate, you're not just a queen waiting for her knight to come. You become the knight and the queen, honey! It's about being able to take the driver's seat and navigate through the economic landscape. Want to start a business? With financial literacy, you'll understand the risk and rewards, and you'll be able to make educated decisions.

And let's talk about investing, the ultimate game-changer. By understanding and engaging with the investment world, you're opening doors to exponential financial growth. You start to see money as a tool, not just a necessity. Investing allows you to build wealth that can be passed down generations, breaking the cycle of poverty and setting your family up for success.

But most importantly, financial literacy empowers us, my Queens! It's about having the confidence to walk into a room and negotiate your worth. It's about making educated decisions that align with your goals. Financial literacy equips us with the knowledge to claim what's rightfully ours.

Now, the road to financial literacy is not paved with gold, but the destination certainly can be. It takes discipline, patience, and most importantly, a commitment to self-education. Yes, my Queens, you're going to have to hit the books and probably attend a seminar or two. But I promise you, it's worth it.

So, let's rise! Let's educate ourselves and create a legacy of financial freedom. We are the change-makers, the trailblazers. We are the queens of our own destiny, and financial literacy is our scepter.

Remember, my Queens, we are not just surviving; we are thriving. Financial literacy is our right and our pathway to freedom. So, let's claim it, let's own it, and let's pass it down to the next generation of Queens. We got this!

Honey, Let's Speak Money: Cracking the Code of Financial Jargon!

Let's dive into a world that may seem like a foreign language, but I promise you, it's not as scary as it seems. Yes, honey, we're talking about financial jargon.

Let's get one thing straight: these financial terms are just words, not some mystical code meant to keep us at arm's length from our own hard-earned money. And I'll tell you what – by the end of this, we'll be speaking this money language like it's our mother tongue!

When we demystify financial jargon, we're kicking down doors, saying, "We're here, and we're ready to take control!" We're dispelling the notion that finance is for the suits in Wall Street. It's for us too, my Queens!

Budgeting, investing, saving, retirement funds – these words may sound intimidating, but they're just tools for us to build our financial empires. And just like you wouldn't step onto a battlefield without knowing how to use your weapon, we're not stepping into this financial war zone without knowing these terms.

Budgeting is nothing more than a map, outlining where our money comes from and where it's going. It's our game plan, keeping us on track towards financial freedom. Investing, that's our seed, honey! We plant it in the right soil (a good investment opportunity), and with patience and care, it grows into a mighty money tree!

And saving – saving is our safety net. It's not about stashing away every penny and living a joyless life. No, ma'am! It's about balancing our present wants with our future needs, ensuring that we're secure today and comfortable tomorrow.

Retirement fund? It's not a one-way ticket to old age, my Queens. It's our ticket to golden years of freedom, where we're not working to live, but living our best lives!

But here's the secret, my beautiful Queens. These are just words until we put action behind them. Just like saying 'I love you' means nothing without showing it, speaking money is useless if we're not backing it up with smart financial decisions.

We're not just going to speak money, ladies, we're going to LIVE money. And by that, I mean living lives where our money is serving us, not the other way around.

Remember, my Queens, our ancestors fought for our right to be educated. They knew the power that comes with knowledge. Now, we're going to honor their fight by educating ourselves financially. We're going to break these chains of financial illiteracy and take our rightful places on our financial thrones.

So, let's crack this code, let's speak this language, and let's own our financial futures. Because honey, when we talk money, we're not whispering – we're roaring!

Girl, Get Fluent: Understanding Key Financial Terms and Concepts!

Ladies, we've taken the first step into our financial journey by deciding to break down that wall of fancy-sounding terms. But, honey, understanding isn't just about memorizing definitions, it's about grasping the concept. And believe me, these ain't no rocket science, it's all about our coins!

Let's start with a biggie, "net worth". Now, I know it sounds grand, but it's quite simple – it's just what you own minus what you owe. Your assets (your cash, investments, property) minus your liabilities (debts, loans, credit cards). It's like the financial mirror – it reflects where you stand today and shows you the way to tomorrow. So, keep a check on it, darling!

Next, we've got "compound interest". Honey, it's your money's best friend! Simply put, it's interest on interest. Say you put $100 in a bank at 5% interest. After one year, you get $5 interest. But the next year, you earn interest on $105, not just your original $100. Over time, this snowballs into a beautiful pile of money.

Now, let's talk about "diversification". Ever heard the saying, "Don't put all your eggs in one basket?" That's diversification. It's spreading your investments across different types to minimize risk. Because, girl, just like we don't trust that one gossiping friend with all our secrets, we don't trust one type of investment with all our money.

And then there's "credit score". Think of it as your financial report card that lenders check to see if they can trust you with their money. The better your score, the more likely you'll get that loan or that credit card. So, pay your bills on time, don't max out your cards, and show them you're a Queen who can handle her finances!

The last term we're covering today is "inflation". This is a sneaky beast. It's the rate at which the cost of goods and services rises over time.

Ever heard your grandma say, "Back in my day, bread was only a dime!"? That's inflation, sweetheart. And that's why we invest – to make sure our money grows faster than inflation, so we're not left with dimes when we need dollars.

My Queens, this is just the tip of the iceberg. The financial world is vast, but not impenetrable. We've got the keys to unlock it and the strength to conquer it. But remember, knowledge is power only when it's applied. So, let's not just learn these terms, let's live them.

We've come a long way, but our journey has just begun. Let's stride into our financial futures, heads held high, hearts filled with determination, ready to claim our financial crowns. Because, ladies, we're not just surviving – we're thriving, and we're doing it in style!

Speak Up, Queen: The Power of Being Informed and Asking Questions

Alright now, ladies, it's time to discuss something crucial. I'm not talking about the latest drama at work or who did what on our favorite reality TV show. No, honey, this is about you, your money, and your future. We're talking about the importance of being informed and asking questions. That's right, girl, I said asking questions. I don't care how silly you think you might sound, your future is worth far more than a few seconds of feeling awkward.

I want to let you in on a little secret. Nobody, and I mean nobody, starts out knowing all there is to know about finance. Heck, even those Wall Street types had to learn the ropes once upon a time. So, let's shed any embarrassment, any hesitation, and get down to business.

Consider this - you wouldn't go to a new hair stylist without asking them about their expertise, right? You wouldn't let them just come at your crown with scissors without checking their reviews, would you? Then why, oh why, would you do the same with your hard-earned money?

Being informed starts with asking questions and seeking out information. Sure, we got Google, and it's a good friend to have, but don't stop there. Pick up books, attend seminars, join finance groups, listen to podcasts, and don't be afraid to ask professionals. Knowledge is your superpower, girl, so get armed and get ready to conquer!

And when it comes to asking questions, don't be shy. This is your money we're talking about. If someone's advice doesn't make sense, ask them to explain it. If you're not comfortable with an investment, ask for alternatives. If you're not clear on a financial term, ask for clarification. No one will look out for your financial health better than you, queen!

Now, I don't want to scare you, but there are folks out there who may try to take advantage of you, especially if they think you don't know the ins and outs of finance. That's why it's vital to be an informed investor and consumer. Your financial literacy is your shield, protecting you from scams and bad advice.

Remember, the goal here isn't just to make money. It's to build wealth, achieve financial freedom, and secure a prosperous future for you and your loved ones. To do that, you need to understand what's going on with your money. You need to be the one calling the shots.

So, let's commit right here, right now, to never stop asking questions, to always strive to learn more. To not just accept what's given, but to reach for what we deserve.

In the world of finance, there's no such thing as a silly question, only silly mistakes that could have been avoided with a little more knowledge. So let's get knowledgeable, let's get powerful, and let's secure these bags, ladies!

Laying the Foundation: Strategies for Wealth Creation and Financial Independence

We've talked about the basics, we've spoken the lingo, and we've learned to ask the right questions. Now it's time to roll up our sleeves and get to the real work - creating wealth and financial independence. This is where we go from simply making ends meet to truly building an empire.

You see, darling, it's not just about making money. Anybody can make money. The true queen knows how to grow her money. We're not just chasing paychecks; we're building wealth. We're looking for financial freedom, the kind that lets us make decisions from a place of power, not desperation.

Now, there's no magic potion here, no get-rich-quick scheme. This is about strategy, patience, and determination. We've got to play the long game. We're talking investments, real estate, and multiple income streams. You've got talents, right? Well, let's put them to use. Start a side hustle, invest in a small business, or purchase property if you can.

Let me tell you something, sisters. Wealth isn't just about having a lot of money. It's about having options. It's about knowing that no matter what life throws at you, you've got a cushion to fall back on. It's about making sure your kids, and their kids, don't have to start from scratch.

And I want you to remember, it's never too late to start building wealth. Whether you're in your twenties, your forties, or even your sixties, you can start making smarter financial decisions today. You've got the power to turn things around.

And let's be real here. It's not going to be easy. There will be sacrifices. There will be risks. But remember what we're fighting for. We're not just doing this for the fancy cars and the designer bags (though those are nice perks). We're doing this for the freedom to live life on our own terms. We're doing this to ensure a better future for our families. We're doing this because we deserve to wear our crowns without worrying about the price tag.

So, let's make a pact right now. A pact to not just earn, but to learn. To invest, not just spend. To think about the long-term, not just the here and now. Let's commit to building our empires, one financial decision at a time.

Remember, queens, this journey is a marathon, not a sprint. Be patient, stay disciplined, and keep your eyes on the prize. And in those moments when you feel like giving up, just remember what you're working for. Your future self will thank you, I promise.

So go on, queen. Build that empire. Create that wealth. You've got the knowledge, you've got the power, and you've certainly got the sass. It's time to take control of your financial future. Let's do this, ladies!

Smart Coins: Investing in Assets, Not Liabilities

Alright, my royal sisters, we've arrived at the real talk part of this money conversation. Now that we've got our sights set on building wealth and creating financial independence, it's time we understand the fundamental rule - investing in assets, not liabilities.

Yes, you heard it right, darling. It's all about owning assets, not liabilities. But let's break it down, so we're clear. An asset puts money into your pocket, and a liability takes money out of your pocket. Simple as that.

Now, don't get it twisted, sweethearts. We all like the shiny things, the designer labels, and the fancy cars. But let's remember - these are luxuries, not necessities. They might make us feel like queens for a moment, but they won't build us an empire.

So, we're not going to throw our hard-earned money at things that depreciate or require constant cash infusions. Instead, we're going to invest in assets - things that will grow in value over time or generate regular income.

Think real estate, stocks, bonds, mutual funds. Think about owning a small business, buying land, or even writing a book that brings in royalties. These are the things that can grow our money, create a steady income, and truly build our wealth.

But here's the thing, queens: investing in assets requires discipline and sacrifice. It means that we might have to say 'no' to the fancy shoes today so we can say 'yes' to financial freedom tomorrow.

Remember this, my beautiful sisters: every dollar we spend is a dollar that could have been invested. So the next time you're about to drop a stack on something that won't bring any return, think again. Is it an asset or a liability? Is it going to bring you closer to your financial goals, or is it going to set you back?

And, listen, I get it. Investing can be intimidating. There's a lot to learn, and there's a risk involved. But don't let that scare you off. Don't let the fear of failure keep you from the potential for success.

You see, queens, the most significant risk of all is doing nothing. It's letting our money sit in a bank account, losing value to inflation. It's spending our money on things that won't bring any return. It's letting our fear of the unknown keep us from taking control of our financial futures.

So, my beautiful queens, it's time to get smart with our coins. It's time to stop feeding our liabilities and start growing our assets. It's time to take a leap of faith, to learn, to grow, to invest.

Remember, we're not just building wealth for ourselves. We're building it for our families, our communities, our future generations. So let's do this, ladies. Let's commit to investing in assets, not liabilities. Let's commit to building our empires, one smart financial decision at a time. Let's show the world what black queens are capable of. Onwards and upwards, my sisters! Let's get this wealth!

Boss Moves: Entrepreneurship as a Path to Wealth Creation

Now, ladies, listen up, because this next topic is a game-changer. We're going to talk about entrepreneurship as a path to wealth creation. That's right, ladies, it's time to step into our power and become the bosses we were born to be.

Look around, my queens. Black women are already the fastest-growing group of entrepreneurs in the U.S. We're shaking up industries, creating jobs, and contributing billions to the economy. But most importantly, we're creating wealth and financial independence for ourselves and our communities.

So what's stopping you? I hear you saying, "But entrepreneurship is risky. What if I fail?" Well, honey, let me tell you something. Failure is not the opposite of success; it's a part of it. Every successful entrepreneur has faced setbacks and failures along the way. But they didn't let that stop them. They learned from it, they grew from it, and they kept going. And you can do the same.

Entrepreneurship is about seeing a need in the market and filling it. It's about using your unique skills, talents, and passions to create value for others. It's about taking control of your time, your income, and your future. And, queens, it's one of the most effective ways to create wealth.

Now, I won't lie to you. Starting a business is hard work. It requires dedication, perseverance, and resilience. It requires you to step outside of your comfort zone and take risks. But, my queens, the reward is worth the risk.

Think about it. As an entrepreneur, you're not just earning a paycheck; you're building an asset. You're creating something that can generate income for years to come. You're creating something that you can pass down to your children and grandchildren. That's what wealth creation is all about.

And don't forget, queens, you're not alone in this journey. There are resources available to help you succeed. From business training programs to networking groups to startup grants and loans - there are countless ways to get the support and funding you need to launch and grow your business.

So, my queens, let's start dreaming big. Let's start thinking about what we can create, not just what we can earn. Let's start seeing ourselves as the bosses we truly are.

Don't let fear hold you back. Don't let the risk of failure keep you from the potential for success. You have everything you need to succeed within you. You have the strength, the resilience, the creativity, the passion. All you need to do is step into your power and claim your crown.

So, let's do this, ladies. Let's embrace entrepreneurship as a path to wealth creation. Let's start building our empires, one business at a time. Let's show the world what black women entrepreneurs are capable of. Because, queens, the future is ours for the taking. Let's go out there and claim it!

Secure Your Bag: Savings and Emergency Funds as Your Safety Net

Alright, my beautiful queens, it's time to address something that often gets overlooked in the hustle and bustle of life, but is crucial to our financial well-being: savings and emergency funds. Now, don't roll your eyes or sigh. I know, the concept of saving may sound tedious or daunting, but hear me out.

You've heard it before: "Save for a rainy day". Well, that ain't just some old, tired cliché. Life has a way of throwing curveballs when we least expect them, honey. Your car might break down, you could have a medical emergency, or God forbid, lose your job unexpectedly. These are the rainy days we're talking about. And in these moments, having a financial cushion can make the difference between staying afloat or drowning in debt.

Let's get one thing straight, queens. Saving is not about punishing yourself or living a life of deprivation. No, ma'am! It's about being a smart queen who knows her worth and protects her future. It's about building a safety net that gives you the freedom and flexibility to make choices that align with your dreams and values.

Think of your savings and emergency funds as your personal financial bodyguards. They're there to shield you from unexpected blows and keep you standing tall, come what may. That's power, honey! That's financial freedom.

So, how do you build this security blanket? Well, it's simple: by being consistent. Start with what you can, even if it's just a small amount. Don't wait for that big paycheck or bonus. Start now, with what you have. And make it a habit. Every time you get paid, pay yourself first by putting a portion of your income into your savings. It's your future, your peace of mind you're investing in.

I know, life happens, and sometimes it's tempting to dip into these funds for that dazzling pair of shoes or the latest smartphone. But remember, queens, our goal is long-term financial security, not short-term gratification. Every time you're tempted, ask yourself: "Do I really need this, or do I just want it?" Learning to distinguish between wants and needs is a powerful financial skill.

And as you build your savings, don't forget to celebrate your progress. Each dollar you save brings you one step closer to financial independence and stability. So, cheer yourself on, queen! You're taking steps towards securing your future, and that's worth celebrating!

Remember, my queens, being financially savvy isn't just about making money. It's about managing it wisely, too. It's about making money work for you, not the other way around. Building a solid savings and emergency fund is a big part of that.

So, let's do this, ladies. Let's commit to securing our financial future by building our savings and emergency funds. Let's empower ourselves with the financial stability that allows us to weather life's storms with grace and poise. Because we are queens, and queens always secure their bag!

The Crown Jewel: The Power of Black Women in Community

Chapter 8

Alright, my sisters, my queens, we've journeyed together through the depths of self-care, the power of time management, and the mastery of financial literacy. We've donned our crowns and claimed our thrones, growing not just as individuals but as a powerful, radiant collective. Now it's time to delve into our most precious asset: our community.

The power of Black women in community is something to behold. We are not just individuals; we are a collective force of resilience, strength, and creativity. A web of sisters, mothers, daughters, aunties, and grandmothers who uplift, protect, and inspire one another.

Our bond as Black women, the sisterhood we share, is our crown jewel. It's the secret sauce, the magic ingredient that makes us unstoppable. It's the loving gaze of your mama that tells you, "You can do this." It's the encouraging nudge of your sister friend who reminds you, "Don't you dare give up." It's the collective cheer of your community as you ascend, rise, and reign.

Each one of us is like a precious gem. Alone, we shine. But together? Honey, together we are a dazzling spectacle of beauty, power, and grace. We are a radiant crown, lighting the way for each other and for generations to come.

But, queens, let's remember this: being part of a community is not just about taking; it's about giving. It's about lifting as we climb, extending our hand to our sisters who are still finding their footing. It's about amplifying each other's voices, celebrating each other's victories, and holding space for each other's pain.

Our unity as Black women is our strength, and it's needed now more than ever. In a world that often tries to silence us, to make us feel small or insignificant, our unity sends a powerful message: We are here. We matter. We rise.

So, let's lean on each other. Let's learn from each other. Let's empower each other. Because together, we are stronger, bolder, fiercer.

Remember, my queens, your crown isn't just for you. It's a beacon, a symbol of hope and resilience for your sisters. It's a testament to the power of Black women, a power that is magnified when we stand together.

So, let's embrace our crown jewel: our community. Let's invest in it, nurture it, and protect it. Because when Black women unite, incredible things happen. Movements are born, barriers are broken, and history is made.

Sisters, our community is our power. Let's continue to uphold, uplift, and celebrate one another. Let's wield our collective power with pride and purpose. Because we are Black women, and together, we are unstoppable.

So, keep shining, my queens. Keep uplifting. Keep empowering. Our sisterhood is a mighty force, and together, we will reign supreme. Because when we embrace our crown jewel - our community - there is nothing we cannot achieve. We rise, we shine, we conquer. Together.

The Power of We: Uniting Our Queenly Forces

We've talked about many aspects of our lives so far, from owning our time, caring for ourselves, to managing our wealth. But there's a gem that outshines them all - sisterhood and solidarity. Our collective power, my loves, is where our real strength lies.

Now, sisterhood, honey, is not just about late-night phone calls and having someone to go shopping with – though that's definitely part of the fun. Sisterhood is that indescribable connection, that thread of shared experience and understanding that only we can truly grasp. It's that magical bond that ties us together, creating a safety net that can catch us when we fall and catapult us to greater heights.

In the face of adversity, we Black women have a history of rallying together, forming a formidable phalanx that refuses to back down. That, my dears, is the power of solidarity. And when we harness this power, we become a force that can move mountains.

Now, let's get something straight. We're not just talking about getting together for brunch or throwing fabulous parties, though, of course, we do those things beautifully. This solidarity we speak of is about the collective effort, the united front we form to confront the trials and tribulations that come our way. It's about creating a network of love, support, and empowerment that lifts us all.

When we tap into our collective power, my sisters, we elevate not just ourselves but each other. We amplify each other's voices, we shed light on each other's struggles, and we celebrate each other's victories.

When one of us wins, we all win. When one of us suffers, we all rally to provide support.

Being a queen is not a solo endeavor, my loves. It's a collective journey, a shared quest for empowerment, growth, and greatness. Our individual successes are beautiful, yes, but our collective triumphs? Oh, they're magnificent.

So let's stand together, my queens. Let's link arms, align our hearts, and march forward in unison. Let's harness our collective power to uplift, to empower, and to conquer. Let's pour into each other, learn from each other, and grow with each other.

Because together, we are stronger. Together, we are bolder. Together, we are more powerful than any obstacle that dares to stand in our way.

So put on your crown, queen, and reach out your hand to your sister. Let's walk this path together, united in sisterhood and solidarity. Because when we stand together, there is nothing we can't achieve.

Always remember, my queens, you're not alone. We are in this together. And together, we are unstoppable. Embrace the power of "we," and watch how our world transforms.

Stand tall, shine bright, and keep those crowns high, my sisters. For we are queens, and together, we reign supreme.

Our Fortitude: The Unyielding Spirit of Black Sisterhood

Our communities, honey, are as strong as they come. We are the epitome of resilience and fortitude. We don't just weather storms, we dance in the rain, pick up the pieces, and keep it moving.

From the dawn of time, Black women have been the pillars that hold up not just our communities, but the world. We are the backbone of society, the nurturers, the fighters, the lovers, the teachers, the leaders, and the builders. We have endured, persisted, and fought for our rights and freedoms against all odds.

And let's get this straight, my queens. Our strength doesn't come from our struggles. No, darling. Our strength comes from how we rise above them, how we grow through them, and how we lift each other up along the way. Our strength comes from our spirit, our heritage, our ancestors, our faith, and our unyielding love for one another.

Our strength comes from the determination in our eyes when we stare adversity in the face and say, "Not today." Our strength comes from the undying hope in our hearts that dreams for a better tomorrow for our children, our sisters, and our brothers. Our strength comes from the wisdom of our mothers and grandmothers, the courage of our fathers and grandfathers, and the fiery passion of our youth.

Look around you, my queen. Look at your sisters, your friends, your neighbors, your colleagues. Look at their accomplishments, their perseverance, their grace, their beauty, their wisdom. That's the power of our community. That's the strength of Black women. That's the resilience that we're made of.

Remember, queen, when life gets tough, when the road gets rough, when the mountain seems too high to climb, you are not alone. You are part of a powerful, vibrant, resilient community of Black women. You are a piece of a beautiful, intricate tapestry woven from threads of courage, wisdom, love, and resilience.

So, darling, when you feel like giving up, remember the strength of the queens who came before you. Remember their trials, their victories, and their lessons. Remember that you are a part of that legacy of strength and resilience.

But above all, remember this: No matter what comes your way, you have a sisterhood of Black women standing with you, cheering you on, and ready to lend a hand.

Hold your head high, my queen, and let your crown shine. Remember the strength within you, the resilience that's in your DNA, and the power of the community that surrounds you. Remember, darling, you are a Black woman, and there's nothing you can't handle.

Stay strong, my sisters. Keep shining, keep rising, keep thriving. And remember, we are all in this together, and together, we are unstoppable. Always remember, my queens, you're not just strong. You are Black woman strong. And there is no force more powerful than that.

The Power of Us: Stories of Triumph through Sisterhood

Now we've established that our community is one of resilience and fortitude, it's time to show and prove. So, buckle up, sis, 'cause we're about to take a ride through the annals of our collective action.

First off, we've got to shout out the sister circles that have held us up for centuries. We've been pooling resources and supporting one another since the days of our grandmothers and their grandmothers before them. Take the concept of Sou-Sou, for example. It's a money-saving method rooted in our West African heritage where a group of trusted folks come together to contribute funds regularly. Every so often, each person gets the total pot. It's not just about the money, it's about the trust, the support, and the community. That's us. That's Black women.

But let's talk about some more recent examples, queens. We can't overlook the power of our sisters in #BlackLivesMatter. Alicia Garza, Patrisse Cullors, and Opal Tometi ignited a global movement, reminding us that our lives matter, our voices matter, and our dreams matter. They rallied millions around the world, forcing nations to confront systemic racism. That's the power of collective action.

Then we have the #MeToo Movement, spearheaded by our sister Tarana Burke. She started a revolution, allowing women, especially women of color, to break the silence on sexual assault and harassment. She used her voice to uplift the voices of millions. That's the power of solidarity.

And, queens, let's not forget our sister Stacey Abrams. Faced with voter suppression in Georgia, she didn't back down. Instead, she galvanized a whole community, leading a massive voter registration drive that changed the face of politics. That's the power of community support.

These are not just stories, queens, these are our realities. These are the threads woven into the rich tapestry of our shared journey. These women, these movements, they didn't rise out of a vacuum. They rose from the strength, resilience, and tenacity that is intrinsic to Black womanhood.

Now, I'm not saying it's always easy. No, my queens, it ain't always a bed of roses. But we've got to remember the strength that comes from unity, from lifting one another, from speaking out for our sisters when they cannot. That's where our power lies.

Remember, my queens, you're not alone. You are part of an indomitable sisterhood, a lineage of women who stood tall, who held their ground, who dared to dream and act for a better tomorrow. That's your heritage. That's your legacy.

So, my beautiful queens, let's keep this legacy alive. Let's keep supporting each other, standing up for each other, and lifting each other up. Remember, we rise together. We shine together. And together, we are unstoppable.

Stay blessed, my queens. Continue to embrace your crown and let your light shine. Always remember, there's power in unity, strength in sisterhood, and victory in collective action. We are Black women, and together, we move mountains.

Passing the Torch: Nurturing Growth through Mentorship and Knowledge Sharing

Now, you know as well as I do that there's a special kind of magic that happens when one sister reaches out her hand to another. That's the beauty of mentorship, the transformative power of knowledge sharing.

Remember that old African proverb, "Each one, teach one"? Well, my dears, it's as relevant today as it was back then. It's all about lighting another's path with the flame of your own wisdom. Each one of us has a responsibility to not only climb but also to reach back and pull others up with us.

Consider the impact mentors have had in your life. Maybe it was that one teacher who believed in you when nobody else did, that neighbor who shared life lessons over cups of sweet tea on the porch, or even that boss who took you under her wing. They changed your life, didn't they?

Now, my queens, it's time for you to be that change in someone else's life. Yes, you. You've got wisdom to share, love to give, and a story that can inspire. You can be the guiding light for a young sister struggling to find her way. And the beauty of it all is that while you lift her up, you'll find yourself rising higher too. That's the power of mentorship.

And it's not just about formal mentorship. It's about knowledge sharing on a day-to-day basis. It's about sharing the lessons you've learned, the mistakes you've made, and the triumphs you've celebrated. Share those with your sisters, your daughters, your nieces. Share them at the dinner table, at the hair salon, at the church, at the workplace. Share, because every bit of wisdom shared is a seed planted for a stronger community.

And let's not forget, queens, mentorship and knowledge sharing is a two-way street. While you guide others, be open to learning from them too. Wisdom doesn't always come from age. Sometimes, it comes from fresh eyes, new experiences, and youthful resilience.

So, my queens, as we embrace our crowns and walk in our royal purpose, let's remember the importance of mentorship and knowledge sharing. Let's make a pact to uplift, to teach, and to inspire.

Embrace the call to be a mentor, a guide, a beacon. Take that wisdom of yours and use it to ignite the spark in another. And be ready to learn, to grow, to evolve with every encounter.

Our ancestors passed the torch to us, and now it's our turn to pass it on. This is our legacy, our strength, our mission. To build, to nurture, to inspire.

Remember, queens, in the kingdom of sisterhood, we rise by lifting others. So let's rise, let's lift, let's shine. Each one, teach one, for our strength lies in our unity and our future in the wisdom we share.

Keep your crowns high and your spirits higher, my queens. Onward and upward we go, together.

Guiding Lights: How Mentors and Role Models Shape Our Destiny

Let's get real about something powerful – the influence of mentors and role models on our journey to greatness. You know, those individuals who seem to have a celestial glow, illuminating the path ahead, making the impossible feel achievable. Those women who leave footprints for us to follow, leading us to a place of growth and self-discovery.

My sisters, just think about it. Consider the mentors and role models who've left an indelible mark on your life, shaping your personal and career development. Maybe it was a fierce auntie, a savvy businesswoman in your neighborhood, or a national figure who, though you never met, stirred a fire in your belly with their passion and determination.

They showed you the ropes, didn't they? Provided a map when you felt lost, offered a gentle push when you needed motivation. They were your personal cheerleaders, celebrating your successes and cushioning your falls.

But it's not just about what they did; it's about what they represented. They were the living, breathing proof that a black woman can thrive in the face of adversity, that she can rise to great heights, and that she can wield her power with grace, dignity, and wisdom.

These mentors and role models – they did more than just talk the talk; they walked the walk. And, my queens, that's the essence of influence. When we see it, we believe it, and when we believe it, we can become it.

Now, it's your turn to be that influence, to be that guiding light. Remember, as a queen, your purpose extends beyond your personal kingdom. Your realm of influence, your ability to inspire and guide, is much more profound than you may realize. Embrace that responsibility. Stand tall, knowing that your actions, your words, your choices, are shaping the next generation of black queens.

So, my sisters, as we stride towards our destiny, let's remember those who guided us and be ready to guide others. It's time to return the favor, to pass the baton, to keep the chain of mentorship alive and thriving.

Remember, the journey to personal and career development isn't a solo mission; it's a relay. We run our part of the race, then pass the baton, ensuring the next runner is in a better position than we were.

You see, my queens, this is how we elevate our community – by climbing and then extending a hand to those behind us. Each one of us has the potential to be a beacon, a mentor, a role model, to inspire a sister to reach for the stars.

So, queens, let's continue to rise, inspire, and uplift. Remember, your story, your journey, could be the guiding light for another sister. So shine bright, my queens, shine bright. After all, as we lift others, we rise higher ourselves. Now that's what I call black girl magic.

Become the Lighthouse: Guiding and Being Guided on Our Journeys

We've talked about the power of mentorship, and how vital it is to our growth. Now, it's time to get down to the nitty-gritty. We're talking about the how – how to find a mentor and, just as importantly, how to become one.

First things first, don't sit around waiting for a mentor to just magically appear. No, honey, you got to be proactive. Make yourself visible. Attend networking events, join professional organizations, get involved in your community. Show up and show out, my queens!

And when you see a sister who embodies what you aspire to, don't be shy! Reach out. Most folks are flattered to be asked for advice. Approach her with respect and genuine interest, and let her know that you admire her journey. Ask her if she'd be willing to share some of her wisdom with you. Remember, closed mouths don't get fed!

Now, let's flip the script. Think about becoming a mentor. Yes, my queens, each one of you has a wellspring of knowledge and experience to share. You might think, "Me? A mentor?" But let me tell you, no matter where you're at on your journey, there's someone behind you who could benefit from your wisdom.

Look around you, in your neighborhood, your workplace, your church, your sister circles. Is there a younger woman, or maybe a peer, who's hungry for knowledge, eager to learn, and could benefit from your guidance? Take her under your wing. Share your experiences, your wisdom, your insight. You have the power to light the way for another queen.

But remember, mentorship isn't about molding someone in your image. No, it's about guiding and supporting them as they blossom into their unique, authentic selves.

And listen, mentorship isn't a one-way street; it's a two-lane highway. While you're offering guidance and wisdom, be open to what you can learn in return. Sometimes, seeing the world through fresh eyes can offer new insights. So, remain humble and open. As much as you're a beacon for others, allow their light to illuminate your path too.

In the end, it all boils down to this – we're in this together. We rise by lifting others. We empower ourselves by empowering others. This is the essence of sisterhood, of community, of unity.

So, my queens, let's continue to inspire and be inspired, to guide and be guided, to mentor and be mentored. Our strength lies not just in our crowns, but in the power we have to help each other adjust them. So, keep shining, keep guiding, and most importantly, keep uplifting each other. After all, there's no force more powerful than a group of determined queens marching in step towards their destiny. Now let's move, sisters, let's move!

Putting Our Coins Where Our Hearts Are: Uplifting Our Communities

We've got more economic power than we often realize, and it's time we start using it to uplift ourselves and our communities. We're not just consumers, we're investors. And I'm not just talking about stocks and bonds, no honey, I'm talking about investing right here, in our communities.

When we spend our dollars at Black-owned businesses, we're not just buying a product or a service. We're investing in a dream. We're fueling an engine of change. We're keeping our coins circulating in our community, lifting each other up. Every dollar we spend is a vote for the kind of community we want to live in. So let's vote for prosperity, for empowerment, for resilience!

Think of it like a garden. If you plant your seeds in fertile soil, water them, give them sunshine, they're going to bloom. It's the same with our communities. Invest in them, nurture them, and watch them flourish.

But remember, community investment doesn't stop with our wallets. Our time, our skills, our wisdom - these are all forms of currency.

Consider volunteering at a local school, offering your expertise to a non-profit, or lending a hand to a sister starting her own business. Or maybe, just maybe, you've been feeling that entrepreneurial spark yourself?

Go on, fan that flame, my queen! Build that business, start that non-profit, launch that initiative. Be the change you wish to see!

Our collective power is immense, sisters. Each one of us is like a drop of water, but together, we form an ocean. An ocean that can erode even the most stubborn obstacles, that can carve out new paths, that can nourish and sustain life.

So, let's make waves, my queens! Let's harness our economic power. Let's invest in our communities. Let's uplift each other.

And let's not forget, every revolution starts with hope. Hope that things can be different, better. Hope that inspires action. Hope that refuses to be extinguished, no matter how fierce the winds of adversity.

This is our hope, my queens. This is our revolution. So let's put our coins where our hearts are. Let's use our economic power to sow seeds of change. Let's stand tall, stand proud, and stand together. Because when we lift each other, we all rise.

So go forth, my queens, with your crowns held high and your wallets open wide. Be the catalysts of change in our communities. Keep that black girl magic flowing, keep those dollars circulating, and keep lifting as we climb. Our communities, our families, our futures depend on it. Onwards, my sisters, onwards!

Circle of Prosperity: Backing Our Black Brilliance

We've tackled self-care, we've explored time management, we've brushed up on financial literacy. Now, it's time to turn that knowledge, that power, outward. It's time to shine that light on our community!

You see, when we support Black-owned businesses, we're not just buying a product or a service. No, honey, we're fueling dreams! We're pouring our hard-earned coins into the businesses that understand us, that cater to us, that represent us. When we invest in Black communities, we're strengthening the roots that hold us up.

We've got to understand that every dollar we spend is like a seed. Plant it in the right place, and it'll grow into a tree of opportunity, of prosperity, of empowerment. So let's plant those seeds in our own gardens, in Black-owned businesses, in our communities.

I want you to imagine a river. That river's course, its power, its impact, they're all determined by where it flows. Now, imagine that river is your money. Direct that flow towards our businesses, our communities, and watch as it carves out pathways of prosperity, as it fuels the growth of a vibrant, resilient, thriving Black economy.

But let's not stop there, queens. It's not just about spending money; it's about investing time, resources, and expertise. It's about lifting as we climb. We've got skills, knowledge, and experience that our communities need. So, let's share that wealth, let's sow those seeds of wisdom.

When we support Black-owned businesses, when we invest in our communities, we're building a legacy, a foundation for the future generations. We're telling our children that they matter, that their dreams are valid, that they can be creators, innovators, entrepreneurs. We're showing them what Black excellence looks like.

And let me tell you, sisters, nothing – absolutely nothing – beats the feeling of walking into a Black-owned business, of seeing our people succeed, of knowing that your support helped make it happen. It's a feeling of pride, of kinship, of hope.

So, let's take up this mission, my queens. Let's turn our economic power into a force for change, a force for progress, a force for prosperity. Let's support Black-owned businesses, invest in our communities, and watch as our collective power transforms our world.

Yes, my queens, we've got this! We've got the power, the resilience, the wisdom to build a circle of prosperity that lifts us all. So, let's get to work. Let's put our money, our time, our skills where they matter most. Let's create a ripple effect of success, of prosperity, of empowerment that reverberates through our communities, through our generations, through our legacy.

So go forth, my queens, with your crowns held high and your hearts full of hope. Let's transform our communities, one dollar, one business, one dream at a time. It starts with us. It starts now. Let's do this, sisters! Let's embrace our crowns, take up our power, and let's lift as we climb. Onwards, my queens, onwards!

Concluding Thoughts: Let Your Crown Shine, Queens!

Chapter 9

Alright, my beautiful queens, we've come to the end of our journey, but oh, what a journey it's been! We've walked through the many facets of our queenhood, unpacked the realities of our time, and emerged, crowns gleaming, ready to seize our thrones. Yes, sisters, we are ready to lead, to thrive, to sparkle!

Now let's reflect on our journey. We started with an examination of our regal anatomy, embracing our poise, our energy, and how we present ourselves to the world. We shattered the myth of multitasking and reclaimed our time, declaring loud and clear that our time is valuable. Our time is sacred.

Then, we understood the art of priority and the importance of investing in ourselves. We dove into the practice of mindfulness, learning to live in the moment, to detox from distractions, and recharge. We learned to relax, reset, flow, and flourish - our mantra for balanced living and leading.

In our exploration of Black America's economic state, we acknowledged the challenges we face, but more importantly, we celebrated the opportunities we have. We're not just workforce participants, honey. We're catalysts for change, pushing our sisters into higher-paying positions, claiming our well-deserved seats at the table.

Our journey into radical self-care taught us to prioritize our physical, emotional, and spiritual wellness. We gave ourselves permission to let go of guilt, to indulge in self-love and self-care without an ounce of remorse. Remember, queens, our wellbeing is our wealth.

Speaking of wealth, we delved into the Queen's treasury, understanding the power of financial literacy. We learned to talk money, to understand it, and to ask the right questions. We plotted strategies for building our empires, investing in assets, embracing entrepreneurship, and safeguarding our wealth.

Then, we came to our crown jewel – our community. We reveled in the power of our sisterhood, in the strength of our solidarity. We celebrated our collective successes and vowed to each one, teach one. We understood the power of mentorship, of sharing our knowledge, and investing in our communities. We learned to back our Black brilliance, supporting our own, fueling our dreams.

Now, as we close this book, I want you to carry its lessons close to your heart. I want you to remember that your crown isn't just an adornment. It's a symbol of your strength, your resilience, your power.

Go forth, my queens, with grace, with poise, with energy. Invest in yourselves, in your wellbeing, in your financial literacy. Seek out mentors, become mentors, support your communities, and let your crowns shine with the brilliance of your potential.

This book may end here, but your journey, our journey, doesn't. We've got crowns to adjust, thrones to ascend, empires to build. So, let's seize our time, embrace our crowns, and rise, queens, rise!

Remember, queens, you're not just wearing your crown; you are the crown. So, keep your heads high, let your crowns shine, and let the world see the power, the brilliance, the resilience of a queen. Let's do this, sisters! Let's seize our thrones, and let's rise, queens, rise!

The Queen's Encore: Marching Forward, Heads Held High

Look how far we've come. From breaking down the mechanics of queenhood to waving our scepters over our financial futures, we've traversed some rocky terrains and scaled some high peaks. We've done it all with style and grace, showing the world what Black women are truly made of – nothing less than star stuff, baby!

Now, as we strut our stuff on this royal catwalk called life, let's not forget the beats we've learned to step to. Remember, multitasking ain't our groove. Instead, we choose to focus, to give each task the attention and care it deserves. We claim our time, fiercely, unapologetically. Remember, time isn't just money; it's power, it's potential, it's our pathway to ascension.

Our journey has shown us that self-care ain't no luxury. It's our right, our duty, our lifeline. We don't just take time for ourselves; we make time, carving it out from our schedules like the precious jewel it is. Our bodies, our minds, our spirits – we care for them, cherish them, treasure them. Because a queen knows that her kingdom is only as strong as she is.

Speaking of strength, we've also learned to flex our financial muscles. We broke down budgeting, investing, and saving, showing Wall Street who's really boss. We learned to translate financial jargon, to ask the hard questions, to take charge of our financial future. Remember, ladies, we ain't just spending money; we're making it, saving it, growing it. Our money's on a mission, and that mission is to build our empires!

As we blaze our trail, let's not forget the power of our community. The sisterhood we share, the solidarity we stand for – these are our strengths. We're not just individuals; we're a collective, a force, a movement. We support each other, lift each other, teach each other. Because when one queen rises, we all rise. That's the power of sisterhood, the power of us.

So, my queens, as we step off this page and into our world, let's carry these lessons with us. Let's walk with grace, with power, with purpose. Let's invest in ourselves, care for ourselves, love ourselves. Let's become the mentors we wish we had, the leaders we know we can be, the queens we truly are.

But above all, let's remember our crowns. Those brilliant, beautiful symbols of our strength, our resilience, our majesty. We're not just wearing them; we're embodying them. Because a queen isn't defined by her crown, but by how she wears it.

So, wear yours with pride, with joy, with confidence. Wear it like the radiant queen you are. Because you're not just a queen on the pages of this book; you're a queen in the story of your life. And that, my dear, is a story worth telling.

Go forth, my queens. Take your crowns, your lessons, your power, and shine. Shine in your workplaces, in your homes, in your communities. Shine for yourself, for your sisters, for your world. Because when a queen shines, she doesn't just light up a room; she lights up a universe. And that, my queens, is a sight to behold. So, let's light it up, queens! It's showtime!

My Final Words: Stand Tall, Rise High, Shine Bright

Listen here, my radiant queens, we've crossed the royal terrain together, absorbing wisdom, collecting gems, and stashing them in the treasury of our hearts. Now, as we close this chapter, it's time to take our steps forward, but remember, every step we take, we do it with purpose, with power, with poise.

Honey, we've dived deep into the anatomy of our regality, recognizing the energy that flows within us, the poise that defines us, and the presentation that makes us unforgettable. We've debunked the myth of multitasking, choosing to bathe each task in the golden light of our full attention. Quality, not quantity, is our mantra. Our time is precious, and it is ours to command.

We've discovered the true worth of self-care, how it nourishes our mind, body, and soul. Investing in ourselves isn't selfish, it's essential!

We've understood that self-care and self-love are fundamental keys to our thrones. They make us, they shape us, they empower us.

Let's not forget our journey into the intricate world of financial literacy, where we transformed our mindsets to see the true potential of our coins. Building empires isn't just about bricks and mortar; it's about smart investing, savings, and understanding the money game.

The power of our community, the sisterhood we hold so dear, has been a strong undercurrent throughout our journey. From collective action to mentorship, from supporting Black-owned businesses to investing in our neighborhoods, we've seen how we rise by lifting each other.

So now, my queens, as we stand at the precipice of our future, let these lessons be the wind beneath your wings. Be that woman who walks with the strength of a thousand queens. Be that woman who knows the power of her time, her love, her money. Be that woman who uplifts her community, who mentors, who invests, who thrives.

Hold your head high, wear your crown with pride. Remember, you are a queen not only because of the crown you wear, but because of the way you wear it. You wear it with courage, with dignity, with joy.

So, rise, queens, rise! Let the world see your majesty, your strength, your radiance. You have the power to change your life, to shape your future, to build your kingdom. Step into your greatness, for you are a queen, born to rule, destined to shine.

Let's rise to the occasion, queens. Let's shine our light on the world. Let's show them what we're made of. Because we're made of magic, of love, of resilience. We're made of stardust, of dreams, of possibilities. And when we rise, we don't just touch the sky; we reshape it. That's the power of a queen, the power of you!

Remember, my loves, you are queens, born to lead, born to shine, born to reign. Your journey doesn't end here; it's only just beginning. Stand tall, rise high, shine bright! You got this, queens!

So, march on, my beautiful queens, with your heads held high, your dreams even higher, and your crowns shining the brightest. Remember, you are loved. You are valued. You are powerful.

Keep shining your light, my queens. The world needs your brilliance, your strength, your love. And remember, I am always here, cheering you on, loving you, believing in you.

I love you so much,

Trenace Carter